Jamie Denbo

John Ross Bowie

HEAT

JOHN ROSS BOWIE's writing has
York Press. His acting credits in
Do We Know? and *He's Just Not*
shows, including *The Big Bang Theory*, two of the three *CSI*
series, and *Glee*. He lives in Los Angeles with his wife and two
children.

D1059372

Heathers

Deep Focus

also available in this series:

Heathers

John Ross Bowie

Series Editor, Sean Howe

Soft Skull Press | an imprint of
COUNTERPOINT | BERKELEY

Copyright © 2011 by John Ross Bowie.
All rights reserved under International and Pan-American Copyright
Conventions.

Library of Congress Cataloging-in-Publication Data

Bowie, John Ross, 1971-
    Heathers / John Ross Bowie ; edited by Sean Howe.
        p. cm.
    1. Heathers (Motion picture) I. Howe, Sean. II. Title.
    PN1997.H41225B69 2011
    791.43—dc22

                                    2011005459
ISBN 978-1-59376-406-7

Cover design by Spacesick
Interior design by Elyse Strongin, Neuwirth & Associates, Inc.
Printed in the United States of America

Soft Skull Press
An Imprint of Counterpoint LLC
1919 Fifth Street
Berkeley, CA 94710

www.softskull.com
www.counterpointpress.com

Distributed by Publishers Group West

10 9 8 7 6 5 4 3 2 1

Contents

Heathers

Heathers

Who is going to want to read a book about *Heathers*? It's not the sort of film that scholars around the world have celebrated—but neither is it so left-field that it's never been critically written about before. It is neither *Battleship Potemkin* nor *Bio-Dome*. The official *Heathers* fan site (heathersfilm.tripod.com) has, as of this writing, not been updated since 1999. Why am I spending all this time on such a niche project, I asked myself. I have kids to feed, for fuck's sake. So I took a respite from self-doubt to poke around on some of the political websites to which I am sadly addicted. The lead on Firedoglake, a funny lefty blog founded by columnist and ex-film producer Jane Hamsher, was on former Colorado congressman Tom Tancredo, who'd just spoken at the National Tea Party Convention. In a subsequent interview with the Dutch newspaper *NRC Handelsblad*, he'd cast barbs at Sarah Palin ("I really don't have this feeling that she's presidential") and John McCain ("nasty, mean . . . particularly unstable"). The Firedoglake columnist, who goes by the name Watertiger, had this to say about Representative Tancredo: "Oh, snap! Who died and left Tancredo Heather Chandler's red scrunchie?"

That last phrase was helpfully hyperlinked to *Heathers'* IMDB page, for the benefit of readers who didn't respond to the reference with a smug chuckle. Smug but surprised: It was a reference to a cult movie, twenty-one years after the film's release. A cult film which, by any estimation, tanked in its initial distribution. The same IMDB page indicates that the film still has not made its money back (this is likely untrue, what with video rentals and such, though difficult to confirm since the production company is now defunct. That production company, New World Pictures, which had been founded a decade before by Roger Corman, went under after one more film with a similar box office performance). Yet here it is, referenced on a progressive political blog that, after analyzing Tancredo's questionable conservative credentials, further wonders, "I guess we'll have to wait and see whether the Tea Party bestows the red scrunchie on someone more . . . politically pure."

Apparently, given its status as a catchphrase in the popular lexicon, I will not have to spend any time discussing the symbolism of Heather Chandler's red scrunchie.

If you put three or more people in a room, there will eventually be gossip, politics, coalition building, and backstabbing. And if there is gossip, politics, coalition building, and backstabbing, there will be a connection to *Heathers*, a vibrant and vicious satire that speaks not just to me, but to anyone who steps back a little and looks at the weird and horrible things people do to each other—in politics, in show business, in families. And the universality of *Heathers* is the subject of this book, as well as how it got deep under the skin of a kid growing up 500 huge miles away from the movie's setting among the suburban lawns of Ohio.

The Natural Answer to the Myriad of Problems Life Has Given Me

Built in the 1920s, it was a dank, sooty, six-story building with an American flag waving from its roof—until an ex-girlfriend of mine stole the flag. There was a coal-burning furnace in the basement, which few students ever saw, but those of us who did were certain that the school was built on *a*, if not *the*, mouth of hell. Somebody once took a dump right in the middle of the northwest stairwell, and it sat there for hours.

Having said all of that, I still enjoyed high school quite a bit. Bayard Rustin High School for the Humanities, located in the Chelsea district of Manhattan, is named for a prominent gay socialist Civil Rights leader and was at the time of my attendance one of the most ethnically diverse schools in New York City. We didn't have a football team—few schools in the city do. (Where would they practice?) None of the kids had that suburban status symbol, the car. (Where would they park?) And while I was certainly not among the beautiful people who went clubbing at the Tunnel or Limelight, I had friends, felt a sense of community, and avoided violence (for the most part; more on that later). In the tenth grade I had my first serious girlfriend to whom I lost my virginity the following summer, and had girlfriends of varying degrees of "seriousness" thereafter. I didn't go dancing, but I went to see bands at clubs like the Ritz or CBGB pretty religiously, from which I came home at ridiculously late hours. I have vivid memories of walking down 44th street at 3 AM when the only other life on the street would be a sewer rat and a Hasid getting a hummer from a bewigged hooker (probably a guy). My mom fought these late night excesses with curfews that I pushed and pushed until they just gradually evaporated. My huge bargaining chip in these negotiations was that I didn't drink, and was in fact aggressively, obnoxiously, self-righteously straightedge. So my hours were crazy—terrifying in hindsight, especially now that I have kids of my own—but I never came home drunk or high, which bought me a lot of leeway.

For a big chunk of tenth grade, I wore a backbrace to arrest my kyphoscoliosis (not *correct*, mind you . . . merely arrest). Honors student? Thank you, no. I spent far too much time listening to records and working on stage crew to hold down anything better than a B to C average. I played no sports. I passed gym solely by making the teacher laugh: Mr. Pedroni admired my Keatonesque (both Buster and Diane) pratfalls as I attempted to leap over the pommel horse, and gamely gave me a B. Thanks, Mr. Pedroni, wherever you are! Wait a second—you got fired for messing around with some of the more athletic boys, and *that's* why I've changed your name for the purposes of this story? Well, that's just as well.

So, yes, in the national nomenclature of the time, probably a nerd, sure, but these tidy classifications didn't seem to apply in New York. Sure, I was nerdy, but girls would have sex with me. Sure, girls would have sex with me, but I was the guy who fixed the VCR when it died in class. Sure, I was the guy who fixed the VCR, but I was cordial with a lot of the popular kids, the children of respected actors and artists, stunning girls in black tights, athletic guys who dressed in Benetton chic.

My key social network was stage crew: I had joined in the tenth grade, drawn to this specialized corps that got to miss classes, wear cool walkie-talkies, and carry keys that could open most of the rooms in the building. Enter Patricia, also on stage crew, bookish, thick, busty, and awkward; we fell in love, had weird, sweaty, virginity-extinguishing sex while watching, of all things, *The Wanderers* (which features a teen pregnancy!). She was infinitely smarter than I was, and history would bear this out when she went to Brown and I went to Ithaca. But at the time, she was prone to horrible mood swings, and long, rambling love letters, and tearful apologies, and all the other things that make a girl irresistible to a certain type of guy who thinks romance is supposed to hurt. "Our song" was the Beatles' "Dear Prudence," a musical red flag if ever there was one. She finally had to fuck somebody else to end our relationship, which was one of those relationships that just refused to die. She graduated at the end of my sophomore year, because your narrator was a *player* who dated seniors. Provided they were clinical depressives.

By eleventh grade I was really involved with the crew, and I ascended to the rank of assistant stage manager. That's the year I met Heather #1 (this is not a metaphor; she was actually named Heather), who at the time was a Mormon, so we didn't have sex—but I do remember making out during *Singing in the Rain* . . . no, wait, worse, it was *It's a Wonderful Life*. She was a voracious reader, and, like me, was in some ways different just for the sake of being different. She had arbitrary sartorial rules, such as the belief that everyone should own one really ugly vest. She loved the Dead Milkmen. We went to see the goofy Frankie and Annette re-tread, *Back to the Beach*, on our first date. I was a nerd in love.

The show we put on that year was *Fiddler on the Roof*, which required massive technical maneuvering (Tevye's house flown into the rafters, a massive lighting rejiggering in order to create the proper atmosphere for the dream sequence in Act One). We even considered using body mics but we dropped them during tech week because of all the interference—the school's (armed!) security guards had walkie-talkies that fizzled in on the Anatevkans's conversations. We also ran all the school assemblies, which could be a daunting amount of work, and when I ran out to adjust a microphone, I was swiftly called "nerd" by my less charitable classmates. That hurt so much that I even quit the gig for a while, but couldn't find anything to approximate the high of opening night—the adrenaline and serotonin rushing in as, surrounded by concupiscent, overly made-up teenagers, you watched your set creation being lowered from the flys. That was my high school: heightened, colorful, like every high school . . . only more so.

Heather #1 broke my heart late in my junior year. We were in different places, hers being, "I'm about to graduate from high school and I need my space," and mine being, "Can I crawl inside your tweed overcoat and stay there?" The breakup really smarted. There's a special kind of intensity to nerd love. All high school relationships have an element of "you and me against the world," but when the two participants view themselves as outsiders anyway, it's *Natural Born Killers* with milder editing. Walking down 59th Street near the park one time, we passed two really well-dressed girls (black leggings under minis, hoop earrings, Elaine-from-*Seinfeld* walls of moussed hair) sitting on a park bench, not bothering anyone. Heather #1 and I both said "JAPs" under our breath and the two girls heard us, and lashed out with "Nerds!" And you know what? Totally within their rights. Some total fucking strangers had made a snobbish (and, frankly, anti-Semitic) remark. Heather #1 and I are lucky we didn't get our asses kicked. And make no mistake, two Jewish American Princess girls could absolutely have kicked my ass.

But it was that same adversarial, us-against-the-world relationship—and I think this is pretty common—that made me feel shipwrecked when my partner in contempt left. I hibernated a little until working up the courage to ask out Heather #2 (again, her real name). She was a looker who divided her time between an awesome brownstone in the East Village and a home in Connecticut. She had been off-limits for all of high school, pursued by many and consistently rebuffing all, dating a guy from Connecticut who happened to be a football player (she detested having him dismissed as a "jock," and I'll honor her preference here). They had broken up around New Year's, and slowly, steadily, we became an item—clearly, she was working through some sort of "what's the absolute polar opposite of a guy from Connecticut who plays football?" thing, and there I was, scrawny, bespectacled, long-haired, and walking around with Jim Carroll's *Forced Entries* in my backpack. Sure, she wouldn't tell anyone about us, but people knew, and I really didn't care because New York when you're seventeen and crazy about a girl is the shiniest place on Earth—it's like ten Ozes. People ask me all the time what it was like to grow up in New York City and for years I wasn't sure what to say. Until I asked them what it was like growing up in Swampscott, Massachusetts, or Chillicothe, Illinois. And then I realized, "Wow, I guess taking a date to the opera when you're in high school is pretty weird. And it's pretty weird that I was thirty before I learned how to drive. And I guess that story about the Hasid and the tranny hooker doesn't really tap into a universal nerve." But, yeah, I took Heather to the opera (my dad had season tickets, couldn't use his pair for *Rigoletto*) and to see *Our Town* on Broadway (Spalding Gray was the stage manager), and we walked through Central Park in the crisp new snow, and nobody bothered us and life was great.

While thumbing through my new issue of *American Film* (your narrator had a subscription, yet still had a girlfriend— *amazing*), I was struck by an article about a dark high school comedy that had been kind of a big hit at the Sundance Film Festival. A great idea, and a funny title. I was between allowances and jobless at the time, and she had a job at the Gap on St. Marks, so actually Heather #2 took *me* to see *Heathers*.

Goddamn, Will Somebody Tell Me Why I Read These Spy Novels

Synopsis and Origins of Michael Lehmann's *Heathers*, 1989

When the film shows up late at night on IFC, it's summarized as follows: "Cool Veronica and her quirky boyfriend topple a high school trio of too-cool Heathers," a synopsis so abridged that it borders on the irresponsible. If you've made it this far in this book, you're probably familiar with the storyline, but to recap: Veronica Sawyer (Winona Ryder) is a junior at Westerburg High in Sherwood, Ohio. She is the only non-Heather in an elite cadre of beautiful girls who rule the school—and are in turn ruled by the beautiful and cruel Heather Chandler (Kim Walker). Veronica is growing restless in her position as the smartest of the mean girls, and she has pangs of guilt over leaving her old friend Betty Finn (Renee Estevez) in the dust of her popularity. "Its just like they're people I work with," says Veronica of the Heathers, "and our job is being popular and shit."

Enter Jason "J.D." Dean (Christian Slater). Recently moved to Sherwood, the son of a clearly unscrupulous (maybe even psychotic) real estate developer, he makes a grand entrance, firing blanks at football-playing goons Kurt and Ram (Lance Fenton and Patrick Labyorteaux), who tease him in the cafeteria. After a brief but intense flirtation with J.D., Veronica follows Heather Chandler to a Remington College party, where she humiliates her by throwing up in the middle of the dorm carpet. Heather Chandler promises to ruin Veronica's reputation—"No one will let you play their reindeer games"— and Veronica is faced with the reality of being on Heather's bad side. Furiously journaling at home later that night ("Killing Heather would be like offing the Wicked Witch of the West!"), Veronica is interrupted by Jason crawling through her window. We cut to them in post-coital bliss, as Jason suggests revenge on Heather Chandler. They break into Heather's house the next morning. Figuring that the punishment should fit the crime, Veronica and J.D. conspire to make Heather Chandler vomit profusely. Veronica makes a cute milk and orange juice mixture—a traditional cocktail with a high "upchuck factor." J.D. simply pours some drain cleaner into a mug, making a big show of his seriousness. Distracted by a steamy kiss, Veronica (mistakenly, presumably) takes the wrong mug in to Heather, and J.D. lets her do it. He dares Heather to drink it, and she does, dying instantly. Jason feigns surprise and entreats Veronica—an excellent forger—to fake Heather's suicide note. But then, after her death, Heather is painted by her peers and school administrators as the kind of sensitive, tortured soul that she most definitely was not. If anything, things are getting worse at school! When J.D. tricks Veronica—or does he?—into killing the football goons by giving her a gun with "blanks" that are actually real, live bullets, she realizes that her new boyfriend is dangerous and, in an oft-quoted line from the film, that "my teen angst bullshit has a body count." Breaking up with him only makes matters worse: Jason devises a scheme to blow the entire school to pieces and make it look like a mass suicide. The film ends with a satisfying comeuppance—in most of our high school revenge plots, as in *Heathers*, we only end up hurting ourselves—and there's a glimmer of hope that with the bad seeds gone, perhaps Westerburg will be a better place to be for Veronica's senior year.

Through good old-fashioned networking and good new-fashioned Facebook, I was able to interview both Daniel Waters, *Heathers'* screenwriter, and Michael Lehmann, the film's director (I've been directed by the latter on a couple of TV and film projects). Both are still very eager to talk about the film that put them on the map.

Waters was born in Ohio but grew up in South Bend, Indiana, a city of about 500,000 people. So why not set this epic high school story there?

"Ohio and Illinois have a certain sheen," Waters explains. "Indiana just has a certain farmer, first-red-state-up-on-the-board-in-every-election . . . there's something hicky about it. There's something more *tabula rasa* about Ohio. Indiana might as well be Kentucky."

He feared that people would just say, "Oh, it's about Kentucky," and dismiss it as a story about gun-toting rednecks. He also felt he couldn't set it in relatively urban South Bend, with its multi-ethnic public schools. *Heathers* works because it's about the trivial problems of the upper classes; if we're wondering whether a race riot is going to break out, then we're less concerned about the students and their "reindeer games." These kids have paté to eat, for God's sake!

Waters will cop to being a nerd, but the nerd "that the nerds would send to the UN" (i.e., the ambassador nerd who could conduct himself properly in the international conference with jocks, stoners, and preppies. This was a position that I, as not just a member of the stage crew but its *leader*, always aspired to). As a junior high student, the "frighteningly weak and pathetic" Waters ran the deadliest of school gauntlets and emerged victorious: He was the last man standing at the end of a game of dodgeball. Of all things. The experience gave him some degree of cred, and probably led to his popularity as a columnist in the school paper (the column was called "Troubled Waters"). High school wasn't nightmarish for him, either, but if you're thin-skinned, if your job is to notice things and write about them, the emotional warfare around you can turn very literal very fast.

Waters had a couple of ideas for his first screenplay—a lesbian version of *Badlands*, Terence Malick's stunning 1973 debut in which a love-struck Martin Sheen and Sissy Spacek embark on a murder spree (like *Heathers*, *Badlands* is anchored by its lead female's narration), and another in which an alienated high school girl starts dating the anti-Christ. He'd also written, while studying screenwriting at McGill University, a short screenplay wherein a high schooler is accused of being a witch and is subsequently burned at the stake under the supervision of three girls who share the same first name. Later, working in a video store, Waters decided he wanted to expand that idea into "the final word in high school films"—and he wanted Stanley Kubrick to direct. Waters really thought he had a chance at getting Kubrick; the reclusive director was known to be a voracious consumer of media, watching sitcoms and even TV commercials to study their craft and find actors to work with. Waters reasons, to this day, that Kubrick was a man of many genres—horror, period piece, science fiction. Ergo, he was due to make a high school film.

The film's influences aren't entirely film-school canonical: Heathers loosely follows the plot of 1976's *Massacre at Central High*. Directed by former Russ Meyer cameraman Renee Dalder, *Massacre* has some striking similarities to *Heathers* (the last act is particularly close, beat for beat), but the earlier film is so devoid of technique, so exploitative (the near-rape victim leaves the scene of her attack, conveniently forgetting to button up her shirt or, indeed, even cover herself) that the two films barely deserve the comparison. *Massacre*'s angle is that once the upper classes are eliminated, the next class down will rise and be corrupted, a valid argument that is handled with much more humor and style in *Heathers*. When considering seeing *Massacre at Central High*, be put off by the slasher movie title. Failing that, be put off by the truly awful soft rock theme song. Failing that, be put off by the bad lighting, boom mic cameos, and wooden acting. And good luck finding it anyway; it's long out of print and I had to download it illegally.

Waters pleads not guilty to improving upon *Massacre*: "I most definitely had not seen the movie, but I do remember reading about it in the beloved book *Cult Movies* by Danny Peary[1] . . . so I guess it was rattling around somewhere in my subconscious. When it was brought up in reviews, my reaction—as well as the rest of Earth's—was 'Huh?' This scares me because I know soon someone will do a *Heathers* rip-off and when they read the comparison in a review, they'll scrunch their face in the same way: 'What's a *Heathers*?'"

Heathers' other interesting antecedent is one of Waters's favorites: the 1968 Anthony Perkins/Tuesday Weld thriller *Pretty Poison*, about the relationship between a young man released from prison after serving time for arson and a vulnerable teen from an unhappy home. He convinces her, almost effortlessly, that he's a CIA agent, and it looks very much like he's going to lead her down the garden path to dissolution. In a neat twist, it's Weld who poses the darker threat, laying the foundation for *Heathers*, two decades later. Weld's work in *Pretty Poison* is pretty stellar; her Sue Ann is a scary specter of manipulation and malevolence wrapped in a naive, all-American package. She's not a cheerleader, no, but in a

---

[1] Peary and 1970s *Time* magazine film critic Vincent Canby are among the apologists for Dalder's film.

sly writerly construct she carries a rifle in her school's drum corps. She's what the parole officer played by John Randolph is talking about when he warns Perkins that he's entering "a very real, tough world. It's got no place for fantasies." She is even what Heather is talking about when she advises Veronica, via voiceover, that "real life sucks losers dry."

Counting on Stanley Kubrick's reputation for gravitating toward epic screenplays, Waters' first draft was 196 pages long (as a rule, screenplays tend to run about a minute per page, which would have made *Heathers* a three-hours-plus film; by contrast, the theatrical version runs one hour and forty-three minutes). Frighteningly weak as I am, I sometimes require both hands to move the 196-page draft from one part of my desk to another. In this first draft, you're over an hour in before anyone dies; you get to see the strip croquet match that's only alluded to in the finished product; and preppie Peter Dawson creates a massive subplot out of an anti-suicide organization called the Genesis Club. There's also the legendary "Prom in Heaven" scene: Veronica kills J.D., but then, seeing all the abuse still going on in the hallways, she lets the bomb blow the school (and herself) quite literally to kingdom come. Smash cut to the last dance, where all the students, regardless of social caste or standing, are partying together, with Veronica gazing upon them beatifically under a banner that reads, "What a Waste, Oh, the Humanity"[2]. Cumbersome and ambitious, this 196-page draft made it to

---

[2] If that sounds familiar, it's not because the ending was ever shot; it's because that's more or less how *Titanic* winds up.

screenwriter Larry Karaszewski[3], who had known Waters in South Bend, and who showed it to his USC classmate, the young director Michael Lehmann.

Lehmann had grown up in San Francisco, a hippie with a deep love of film nurtured at the nearby Pacific Film Archive. In high school, he got what he calls "a really good taste of girl-to-girl cruelty": In the summer before ninth grade, his older sister was diagnosed with Hodgkin's disease and had to take the first year of high school off for treatment. Her friends turned on her, spreading rumors that she was absent due to a pregnancy. "People that I knew," he marvels, "friends of mine, who I liked, would say nasty things about my sister just because it was fun to be mean. And that was disturbing." Add to that two friends who killed themselves in high school, both out of the blue, both obviously unforgettable. "Being a fundamentally superficial person, I didn't take it all that deeply but . . . I felt that, and this is something *Heathers* goes into in depth . . . grownups didn't get it."

Lehmann's student film, *Beaver Gets a Boner*, was about a hardworking kid who needs a college scholarship so he can pay off his drug supplier (the charmingly crass film's highlight is a scene in which our hero sells heroin to a boy scout). On the strength of that, Lehmann had secured a development deal with the struggling New World Pictures. That independent studio released arguably the finest films associated with Roger Corman—*Big Bad Mama*, *Death Race 2000*, and *Rock'n'Roll*

---

[3] Karaszewski, a great screenwriter himself (*Ed Wood,* among others) has apparently never lived down giving Waters the note, "Do they all have to be named Heather?"

High School, to name just about the best triple feature an exploitation fan could pray for. But by 1983, Corman had sold the company and the output had softened to movies like the Sarah Jessica Parker teen vehicle *Girls Just Want to Have Fun* and the horror spoof *Transylvania 6-5000* (a film that has one decent joke, and you've just heard it). But New World also released the seminal *Hellraiser* films, which to a certain type of cultist, at least, started out as smart, scary, and magnetic.

Lehmann had cut his production teeth assisting Francis Ford Coppola on *The Outsiders* and *Rumble Fish*, the latter an underrated impressionist gem of adolescence. He fell quickly in love with Waters's *Heathers* script and passed it on to Denise DiNovi, who had been New World's executive vice president of production and was now looking to make a big, controversial splash in her debut as a producer. He then called Waters with some notes and suggested cuts. Waters would have none of it. *Who is this USC kid*, he asked himself, *when I am—I know in my heart—going to get Kubrick to direct my work?* Lehmann patiently asked Waters, if he were unable to secure the director of *Barry Lyndon* and *Dr. Strangelove* for his first screenplay, would he please consider attaching Lehmann?

Waters was twenty-five, Lehmann thirty. Principal photography began in the spring of 1988, starring sixteen-year-old Winona Ryder, who'd had to be pushed on New World. They feared she wasn't glamorous enough, having only seen her in what everyone had only seen her in—as the geeky girl in *Lucas* and the proto-Goth in *Beetlejuice*. Lehmann, though, saw in her a Natalie Wood quality. For J.D., the producers passed on the "too nice" Brad Pitt in favor of Christian Slater; for Heather

Duke they cast against type a sweet-faced actress best known for her recurring role on *Little House on the Prairie*, Shannen Doherty. And with that, the film's damn near perfect ensemble snapped into place like a bullet entering the chamber.

Not long before the film commenced shooting, Steve White from New World asked that the ending—the Prom in Heaven—be changed. "His point," Lehmann recalls, "was that as a responsible film executive, he couldn't really make a movie that was a satire dealing with teenage suicide in which the character that we *do* identify with kills herself, and kills other people." White feared being blamed for copycat suicides, which Lehman dismisses: "If a kid commits suicide after seeing a movie, then they were going to commit suicide anyway. Their problems go much deeper than the hour and a half they spent in a theater . . . Our feeling was, you can't draw that direct causal connection, and you shouldn't, and you shouldn't have your work be determined by that fear. But we weren't 'responsible film executives.'" White (no tight-ass executive cliché—he'd studied with the famed LA sketch comedy group the Groundlings and had overseen the first TV movie about AIDS) promised to keep other requests for changes to a minimum. But the massive murder-suicide at the end had to go. The only other studio that expressed interest in the film was New Line, which was making a mint on the *Nightmare on Elm Street* franchise—but they wanted to spend less money and ask for more changes. Yes, the company that brought you Freddy Krueger wanted to tone down *Heathers*.

There were other little tweaks along the way: The character of Veronica is *much* more complicit in the murders in earlier drafts—she consciously poisons Heather Chandler, she electrocutes Peter Dawson in the Genesis Club story arc; Waters describes her as "Travis Bickle in a Molly Ringwald package"—but by the final draft she has turned into, if not an innocent lead astray, at the very least a manslaughter practitioner with basically good intentions. Regarding the Veronica of the finished film, Waters laughingly calls her the "Albert Speer of Westerburg High," noting that, like Hitler's architect, she never actually had anything to do with killing, but was part of the aesthetic, the look, the camaraderie of tyranny . . . and loved benefiting from the power. Waters himself softened Veronica when Ryder was cast, due to the "wobbly" (a word he's fond of) quality that she brought to the heroine. That wobbliness leads us to root for her despite the fact that she does willingly shoot Kurt (more on that later).[4]

Lehmann speaks wistfully of Waters' crestfallen reaction to some of the changes, but likes his adjustments, calling him "the most inventive, flexible writer I've ever worked with." When the Southland corporation balked at the use of their 7-11 chain, Waters swiftly created the Snappy Snack Shack and changed the Slurpie to a Slushie.

Lehmann has never viewed the film's ending as a sincere note of hope. His "tongue was way up in [his] cheek," he says; he doesn't think it was a "really happy ending, it's just

---

[4] Ryder has that effect on Waters. In his last directorial effort, *Sex and Death 101*, she plays a woman named Death Nell who serially puts her male victims into comas (a serial coma-inducer), and her character is made much more palatable by her warm, vulnerable, and yes, wobbly performance.

an ending that avoids total destruction." (I respectfully disagree—more on that later, too).

"I've come around on the ending," Waters said recently, "especially now that I talk to a lot of teenage girls and women growing up [at the time of *Heathers'* release]. The fact that Veronica doesn't die, the fact that it doesn't end in violence, was a good thing for them."

One alternate ending—never scripted, but pitched after shooting had commenced—starts just the way the current one does. But after J.D.'s death, when Veronica asks the eternal victim, obese Martha "Dumptruck" Dunstock, to hang out and "rent some new releases," Martha pulls out a gun, says, "Fuck you, Heather," and shoots Veronica in either the stomach or the mouth, depending on when Waters is telling the story. Veronica, spitting up blood, burbles out again and again, "My name's not Heather . . . my name's not Heather . . ." while Martha, in one final salute to Kubrick, stands up from her wheelchair, triumphantly announcing, "I can walk," à la Dr. Strangelove.

Are You a Heather?

Naming and Signifiers in *Heathers*

Heathers is a weird beast: a fluffy black comedy, a brightly lit confection that gestures toward depth (and occasionally delivers), and an eerily timeless morality play. It begs to be taken seriously—and then seems to mock us for doing so. This script is a tour of the highs and lows of American culture. Embedded within are references to the perennial *Archie Comics*, with its Cain-and-Abel duo Veronica and Betty; Mark Twain's most carefree hero, Tom Sawyer; '80s college rock icons the Replacements and their lead singer Paul Westerberg[5]; and Sherwood Anderson's Joycean story cycle *Winesburg, Ohio*. All are deliberate; all mean something. Our heroine is named Veronica Sawyer, not Betty Finn—she's not the chaste good girl from the *Archie Comics*, Betty Cooper, and she's not Huck Finn, the guy who liberates the slave, however temporarily. She's the black-haired temptress, Veronica Lodge, merged with the insouciant prankster, Tom Sawyer. The insouciant prankster who lacks a real moral compass, and not the noble, fighting-against-the-odds Finn, whose book is a staple of twelfth grade reading lists. Because, simply put, Finn is better for you than Sawyer.

---

[5] The spelling change was not originally intended; Waters was asked by producers to change the "e" to "u" since Westerberg sounded a little too Jewish for a suburban Ohio high school.

Veronica's trapped in a high school named for the Midwest's greatest indie rock poet, Paul Westerberg, whose first four or five albums with the Replacements are required '80s alienation music. On the 1982 *Stink* EP, Westerberg gave us the verse-chorus progression:

> They laugh in the middle
> of my speech
> Swingin' in the hall
> Out of reach
> Learning learning who can take
> Talk talk talk talk talk
> Fuck school fuck school fuck my school!

At least, those are the lyrics that can be made out in between primal screams. These words are not supposed to be an articulate indictment of our education system, just a raw spleen-venting about how school can make you feel.

The movie's setting of Sherwood, Ohio casts a respectful nod toward Anderson's dense story collection, which was written after the author suffered a nervous breakdown while running a paint company in Elyria, well outside of Cleveland. Fleeing to Chicago from a small town, he wrote a dizzying collection of short stories set in fictional Winesburg, peeling back the onion layers of small-town judgment and hypocrisy. In one tale, Anderson paints a stunningly bleak portrait of telegraph operator Wash Williams. The "ugliest man in town" is hardly an innocent victim: Underneath his fat, unsightly girth beats a misanthropic heart, burned black by a philandering wife and

her pimpish mother. The story ends with the mother casti-
gating the daughter and stripping her naked in front of her
cuckolded husband. The husband, mad with grief, strikes the
mother with a chair. The story is called "Respectability."

Calling the town Winesburg might have been too glaring
a reference, too on-the-nose. Sherwood will do just fine—plus
there's the added bonus of the Sherwood Forest reference,
since Jason is, no question, killing the rich. (However, since
there are no really poor people in the film's Sherwood who
might benefit from any spoils of J.D.'s crimes, his motives are
questionable at best.)

Names obviously carry a ton of significance in this script,
and I remember this being the first film where I really paid
attention to the, dare I say, "text" of a movie. And I also remember that the Betty and Veronica thing was pointed out to
me by someone else. Maybe even Heather #2. So this was my
first time dealing with film analysis—maybe even semiotics.
For it's not just the borrowed names that are important, but
how they are re-appropriated within the film itself. Forging
signatures is a theme that comes up throughout the film; a
forged signature helps introduce Heather Chandler's cruelty,
and another one covers up her murder. But that word, "forge,"
means a few other things besides "to fake." It also means to
build, create, construct. And we start to forge our identities
in high school—which is what makes these "forgeries" so sinister: Heather Chandler fakes a mash note from Kurt Kelly to
Martha Dumptruck; Heather Duke, stepping gracefully into
Chandler's vacancy, plays the same mash note prank later in
the film; and then J.D. sends Veronica a note that mimics

her own penmanship—as if to say, "I can pretend to be you." These children have barely come to understand who they are before people start absconding with their names, their voices, and their identities.

What a film professor of mine called the "name game" doesn't end there, not by a long shot. The name Heather is Middle English in origin, it's the name of a Scottish flower. According to the U.S. Census, it was virtually unheard of as a first name until 1935, then had a steady climb of commonality, peaking in the early 1970s as the third most popular girls' name in the United States. If you were born in the early 1970s, that means that, like me, like these characters, you were in high school in the late 1980s. The name's popularity has dropped considerably since then; it seemed like every third girl was named Heather when I was growing up, yet I don't know anyone who's naming their kid Heather now. We likely have Lehmann and Waters to thank for this sharp decline.

In their pop-sociology book *Freakonomics*, authors Steven D. Levitt and Stephen J. Dubner point out a "tantalizing" (their word) trend among girls' names. According to birth certificate data for every California child born since 1961, they say, certain names are more conspicuously white, more conspicuously high-income, more conspicuously reflective of the parents'—the namers'—higher education. But that data is very fluid.

Levitt and Dubner make the following assertion:

> There is a clear pattern at play: once a name catches on among high-income, highly educated parents, it

starts working its way down the socioeconomic ladder. Amber and Heather started out as high-end names, as did Stephanie and Brittany. For every high-end baby named Stephanie or Brittany, another five lower-income girls received those names within ten years.

They even have a chart to back it up—and it shows how Heather went from being a respectable ninth most popular "white girl" name in 1980 to a number two ranking in the "low end" of white girl names in the 1990s. *Heathers* captures a moment in time when to be a Heather of high-school age was to be rich, white, and full of hope. Twenty years later, being named Heather in the years between ninth and twelfth grade could mean something else entirely. In the United States, anyway—overseas the film was released with the horribly non-specific movie title *Lethal Attraction*[6], which sounds like one of those horribly non-specific movies that

Vincent from *Entourage* always stars in. In Europe, the name Heather apparently doesn't necessarily connote privilege and wealth. It's just a Scottish plant.

The Heathers' last names are key to understanding them as well—the regal-sounding Chandler, which also echoes the shadowy tales of Philip Marlowe–author Raymond Chandler, and the royal but still

---

[6] Waters and Lehmann liked to joke that the film should be called *Fatal Weapon*.

not-quite-in-charge Duke. And then there's the cheerleader, Heather McNamara, who is named for John F. Kennedy's defense secretary and chief Vietnam strategist, Robert McNamara. "I wanted the guy who was not the top guy, but who was one of the architects," explains Waters, who had read David Halberstam's epic Vietnam account, *The Best and the Brightest*, just before writing the *Heathers* screenplay. "Although Bob McNamara definitely . . . had a lot more going on upstairs." A *cheerleader* named for the man who negotiated the waters of Congress to escalate the war, who allegedly knew about the harmful effects of Agent Orange, and who didn't recant his position until years later. Years after the making of *Heathers*, even.

And our lone wolf anti-hero, Jason Dean, sometimes called J.D., calls to mind iconic rebels and then iconic reclusive authors, all without explicitly hitting the nail on the head. (In an early draft of the script, Jason carries a *Rebel Without a Cause* lunchbox, hitting the nail so squarely on the head as to split the wood and render the whole 2x4 useless.) But the idea isn't to flatter the character by giving him a name so close to the star of *Giant*. "I have a thing against these Jarods, Jasons, Joshes," Waters says, which leads me to quickly protest that I'm a John. Waters clarifies: "John and Jack. *Those* are names. And James is a real name, too. Probably if I was writing the script today I'd call him Joshua Dean, but Jason seemed like . . . I'm kind making fun of the J.D. character in that he's like eighty mimeographs of James Dean and this is what you've got. You've got this wobbly, not quite right, off version of, 'Oh, we're down to Jason Dean now!'"

Real Life Sucks Losers Dry

Bullies and Their Victims in *Heathers* (And Elsewhere)

As I've said, high school was not that brutal for me. But the city itself—New York under Mayor Koch, under Mayor Beame before him—could be rougher than any high school. Bullies exist everywhere in the city. The city can be a bully, itself. My mom and I twice came home to find our small two-bedroom apartment broken into. I was mugged for the first time at age eight. When you're mugged at eight, all your assailants get is one dollar and a library card. But it happened again—punched by strangers, marked (correctly) as passive and non-threatening, and then assaulted, wallet stolen, shoved up against a wall, hit just because I could be.

I've never told anyone this story in its entirety, let alone written it down: I am in ninth grade, and one weekend I'm coming up from the subway with my friend Ben and out of nowhere, five African-American kids come hurtling down the skinny hallway, reaching into our pockets. Ben's off like a shot, scurrying to the token booth, while I swat these children's hands out of my pocket. None of them are taller than I am, except for one—in my mind, he was 6'13" or something, but in reality he was probably only about 5'10". Understanding that I'm putting up a fight, and that no money will be gotten today, the tallest one punches me, a sailing blow to the cheek that knocks my glasses off and almost instantly swells up that side of my face. I stagger back to the token booth, where the insulated clerk calls the cops and has us fill out an "incident report." Into which I, channeling misdirected rage, drop a racial slur. Yeah, your author just told you that he wrote the "n" word on a public document when he was fourteen, and I'm afraid the story gets worse. The cops arrive—two Sipowiczes, one actually fat, bald, and mustachioed—and drive us to the precinct in a squad car. We fill out more forms and then they take us to the public housing right near where we were mugged. It was dark in the subway corridor; it all happened very fast. I don't recognize anyone, so slam—back into the squad car, just to drive around the neighborhood and "see if we see anyone."

We do. They have nothing to do with us at all, but two black kids break into a sprint when they see the cop car and go dashing into a nearby parking lot. The squad car bangs a knife-sharp left into the lot, and both cops are out, *guns fucking drawn*. One kid has vanished, hopped a fence, something, but one kid is under the car, and very, very hesitant to come out. He does, and the cops put him in the backseat. Handcuffed, between Ben and me. The cops then begin to dole out questions: "Where you running to, brother?" "Why'd you take off when you saw us?" And when the kid won't answer, they start putting on a show—for our benefit—as if to say, "Hey, we didn't catch your black guys, but at least we can fuck with this one."

"What if I'd shot you? What if I'd shot you in the leg, huh? Can't play no b-ball no more. What if you get one of those trigger-happy lady cops who shoots you in the dick? Then you can't play basketball, or fuck. What good's your life?"

It goes on like this until, absent any charges, they let the kid go. Keeping my head down, I step out of the car, so he can get out, be un-cuffed, set free. We drive back to the precinct, where my mom, who's been called a while ago, sits on a bench on the verge of tears.

Bullies, all of them. The five kids who tried to mug two, the kid who punched me, the punk middle-class bitch who wrote down "nigger" in a police report, the cops who drew guns on a kid for the felony of simultaneously running and being black. Bullies are not limited to any particular gender, or race, or economic status. So I both laugh and shudder when I watch the bully scene after Heather Chandler's funeral.

The funeral itself is ridiculous: Heather looks stunningly gorgeous in death, the priest lectures the attendees on the dangers of "MTV video games," and Ram silently asks God, "Why'd you have to kill such hot snatch?" On the church lawn immediately following the service, Kurt and Ram are planning a double date. A geek, identified in the script as "Braces," "obliviously steps on Kurt's Foot." The scene continues (the script differs slightly from what made it to screen):

KURT

That pudwapper just stepped on my foot.

RAM

Let's kick his ass.

KURT

Cool off, we're seniors.

RAM

Goddamn Geek!

BRACES gives them "the finger."

BRACES
(*awkwardly defiant*)
Sit and spin.

*KURT and RAM turn to each other more amused than
angered.*

KURT

That little prick.

*The bolting Jocks effortlessly catch BRACES and put him into
a hunched-over position. The other Geeks look on, ashamed.*

KURT

All right you piece of shit fag, do you like to
suck big dicks?

BRACES

Cut it out!

RAM pushes BRACES down harder.

KURT

Say it man. Say I like to suck big dicks.

> RODNEY
>
> Leave him alone, Kurt . . .
>
> RAM (O.S.)
>
> Say it!
>
> BRACES
>
> Okay, okay, you like to suck big dicks.
>
> *Unamused, RAM throws BRACES to the ground. BRACES
> semi-cries.*
>
> BRACES
>
> I like to suck big dicks. Mmm-*mm*! I can't get
> enough of them. Satisfied?

As well as this scene reads on paper, it cooks on screen. First off, kudos to the actor playing Braces—Curtiss Marlowe—who takes the vague stage direction "awkwardly defiant" and makes it seem like the simplest of instructions. You read "awkwardly defiant" on the page and think, "What does that even mean?" Then you see Marlowe perform it and you think, "Well, look at that, that's awkwardly defiant." His delivery of "sit and spin," at a time when a mumbled "sorry" would have spared him a lot of pain, is quixotic in its courage. "Okay, okay . . ." he replies while in one of those unforgiving wrestling holds, and then provides the movie with a terrific misdirection—"You like to suck big dicks." Even though he gets slammed into the ground and has to eat shit within seconds, it's a glorious moment of wish fulfillment, and it's even more satisfying with repeated viewings, when we know that Braces is going to live to the end credits. Kurt and Ram less so.

We spend a lot of the film looking up at the characters—they're looming over us, whether they're forging a suicide note or trapping Braces in a wrestling hold. The camera's right below Braces's face, staring up at an imposing tableau: Braces, Kurt, Ram, and Rodney (another geek) and a huge stone cross closing out the immediate center. This is the vision of *Heathers*: everyone—nerds, bullies, church—they're all piling up on us. We cannot breathe without someone smushing our faces into the lawn of a church. (Add to that the fact that it is in this scene and this scene alone that we can make out some telltale palm trees in the corner of the frame; it would have been great if it had actually been filmed in Ohio, but the bullies in the budget office kept the filmmakers in Sherman Oaks, CA, near the mall where they shot *Valley Girl*.)

Kurt and Ram's deaths are pretty expertly set up: We know that Jason fires blanks, that's been established, and we know that Kurt and Ram have done the unthinkable, running around school claiming to have "had a little sword fight" in Veronica's mouth. J.D. pulls together a collection of gay paraphernalia (or what is taken for gay in Sherwood, Ohio; mineral water is the smoking gun of their sexuality) and then tells Veronica about his "ich lüge" bullets. German speakers have the joke spoiled for them: "ich lüge" means "I lie," and in a creepy turn, after Jason has shot Ram and Veronica has shot Kurt, Veronica lets on that she knew more than she admitted earlier. "Ich lüge bullets. I'm an idiot," she proclaims. Not asking what "ich lüge" means. Just saying, "I'm an idiot." Could she have known? Could her denial about J.D.'s (and her own) intentions be so deep that she could shoot Kurt in the chest and honestly think he'd live? This scene, in the car after the murders, features the satanic moment when Veronica, in a fit of teen self-harm, burns the palm of her hand with the car lighter. And J.D., the devil, lights his cigarette off our heroine's stigmata—her burning palm. If it's an imperfect stigmata, keep in mind that Veronica is an imperfect heroine.

Back to the church lawn: It's a striking, microcosmic scene, and it seems even sharper once you hear who the filmmakers were aping. As mentioned, if you talk to Michael Lehmann or Daniel Waters about *Heathers*, you'll hear the name Stanley Kubrick a lot. Waters's dream director and one of Lehmann's inspirations, Kubrick hovers distantly above the film like a muse. You have to have it pointed out to you, but once you do, you think, of course! Look at the claustrophobic cafeteria scenes: The bright white light invokes the barracks in *Full Metal Jacket*, released just a year before *Heathers* began shooting. That haze through Westerburg's long halls echoes the ethereal dust of *Barry Lyndon*. The frequent use of low, wide angles throughout the movie also bears Kubrick's fingerprints. Look at Braces's comeuppance above, or Jason and Veronica forging the first suicide note, or the wickedly sharp faculty conferences, all shot from below, as if the viewer is laid out on the slab of the huge table: They now reek of the war room in *Strangelove*. And all of that's great, and I love Kubrick, too, but I came of age in the 1980s, and I want to talk about John Hughes.

Hughes had just died when I started the interviews for this book, and he came up pretty organically in the discussions. If the decade began in all its '80s-ness with *Sixteen Candles* (1984), it most assuredly ended with *Heathers*, just as "Morning in America" turned into long afternoons watching the Iran-Contra hearings. *Sixteen Candles*'s heroine Samantha's chaste longings can morph into Jason's homicide and, worse yet, Veronica's complacent complicity. Is *Heathers* an angry rebuke to *Sixteen Candles*'s idealism? *Breakfast Club*'s mawkishness? *Ferris Bueller*'s consequence-free wish-fulfillment? Lehmann is gentle with Hughes:

> When John Hughes started to make his films, I always thought they were clever and funny and entertaining, and I had no problem with that. I think he's a genius and great. But I also found them irritating because they presented what I thought was a whitewashed fantasy view of teenage life that—the kind of anxiety and kind of issues that his characters dealt with were . . . I mean they were real and I think everyone related to them, but they were still sanitized somehow. Nobody took drugs. Nobody *really* took drugs in John Hughes's movies.[7] They had a very colorful but very PG-13 language. And that was so different

---

[7] We can assume Lehmann's qualification is because of the pot scene in *Breakfast Club*, in which five strangers smoke weed together and no one falls into a pit of paranoid despair. Except for Claire (Molly Ringwald), who snaps out of it pretty quickly.

from what my experience of being a teenager was, I didn't buy it. I wanted to show the other side of the John Hughes world. Not that I didn't like that world, but I wanted to show a darker vision of it.

Waters's past interviews presented him as a man trying to correct the perceived damage that John Hughes had inflicted on the world. The Waters of the twenty-first century has softened on Hughes, and he gives it up for the man who "took teenagers as seriously as they did themselves." But he dismisses *The Breakfast Club*'s assertion that "when you grow up your heart dies" with a canned but heartfelt, "Your heart dies when you're ten."

So if your heart dies that early, the adults in *Heathers* are even worse than the ones in Hughes's movies—movies where occasionally Paul Dooley steps in to make everything all right and even Harry Dean Stanton can be superdad (not two years after appearing as a coke-addled Obi-Wan in *Repo Man*). The adults in *Heathers* have completely checked out. They're either robotic, bureaucratic principals or touchy-feely hippies who miss the point in an entirely different way (the smoke-filled faculty meetings illustrate this hilariously, and are as good as any similar board meeting in *Network*). Lehmann, commenting on the suicides of his high school friends, says, "The experience of adolescence is that adults don't understand. That somehow, yeah, okay, they must have gone through it themselves, but where is that pill that they swallowed that makes them forget everything as soon as it's over?" Hughes's parents, with the exception of the cardboard

no-shows in *The Breakfast Club*, seem to remember that their kids are going through a hard time.

The sad thing is that no one seems to have thought to ask the ever-reclusive Hughes what he thought about *Heathers*. Did he laugh? Did he cringe? Did he stare at it vacantly? Did he smack his forehead and think, "What have I wrought?" Was he offended? And if so, did he realize that he had some fucking nerve being offended by anything after bringing the world *Sixteen Candles*'s Long Duk Dong? But this writer likes to think that there's room for all these visions of high school. This can sound like meek equivocation, but there's truth in *Sixteen Candles*, there's truth in *Ferris Bueller*, and occasionally even in *Breakfast Club* (although my favorite scene, tellingly, has always been the moment between the adults—the janitor and Dick, the vice principal—which ends with the janitor blackmailing Dick. There's a real desperation between the two men, for unlike the teenagers upstairs, these guys do not have their whole lives ahead of them). But go back for a second to that moment above: Braces is below the jocks, and we're below Braces, so we have no choice but to sympathize with the downtrodden. Viscerally, passionately. Now check out the *Ferris Bueller* DVD commentary, where Hughes justifies the inclusion of Cameron the killjoy in his Chicago good-time odyssey: "I always had my girlfriend . . . and some guy in the backseat saying, 'What're we doin'?'" Watch your backs, geeks of America: Hughes very well might not have been the peer you think he was.

Color Me Impressed

No one person can or will take credit for *Heathers* working as well as it does. An email exchange with Lehmann and Waters regarding a couple of set-dressing details results in both of them crediting the art department (Kara Lindstrom and Jon Hutman) for the rich, specific details, although Waters does take responsibility for one prop: He insisted that the book on Heather Chandler's table be not Sylvia Plath's *The Bell Jar*, but the CliffsNotes for *The Bell Jar*. The screen is packed with fun treasures that reward repeated viewings—sometimes just jokes, sometimes totems that illuminate character.

The film begins with the nightmarish image of the title characters playing croquet, knocking the enormous wooden balls into Veronica's head. She's buried up to her neck in her own backyard and begins the film's narration from there. Interesting choice, croquet. Not a lot of Americans know how to play it (too European), and it is unquestionably a rich person's game. Think of how many times golf has been used as an expositional device to connote "reckless privilege" or "upper class malfeasance." Think of how many times a director has placed his villain on a golf course so we *really* know that this guy is not just evil, he's fucking loaded *and* evil. Off the top of my head, without double-checking on the Internet: *The Constant Gardener, Goldfinger, Hostel: Part II, Avatar*. Now, having conducted an informal poll of Twitter followers and Facebook friends: *Casino, Falling Down, The Informant, Fahrenheit 9/11*. "Rich bad guy on the links" counts as a time-honored cinematic trope. Now, what's a more nefarious, elitist sport than golf? How about a sport that requires an enormous backyard to have a proper match? How about a sport where you can legally knock another player's ball off the green? How about a sport that has been called the Queen of Games? The croquet court is set up in the backyard of our heroine, but it's Heather Chandler who really excels at the game. And when Veronica, seeking redemption, invites Betty Finn over to play, Finn starts winning, but Veronica quickly overtakes her. At the crucial point when she could knock Betty's ball off the green, Veronica relents, and foreshadows the film's ending. She, in effect, pardons Betty. If you're in dire need of a literary antecedent, the Red

Queen also hosts an eerie, cruel version of the game in *Alice's Adventures in Wonderland.* We'd be fools not to notice croquet's regal—and malevolent—implications.

Speaking of green and red, no discussion of *Heathers* is complete until we talk about the film's use of color. Is it just vulgarly symbolic? Are we supposed to look at Heather Duke's green ensemble and snort "Ah-*hah*! I get it, I was an English major! She's *envious*!"? According to Daniel Waters, no:

> So I have three characters named Heather, and I put their last names on everything, but it was kind of like . . . it just became a major concern of mine to make sure you knew the difference between them at all times. And so anything I could do to highlight the difference . . . Maybe it has a utilitarian purpose in the script, but then when you see the film, it's like, "Ah! They really took that ball and ran with it . . ."

But any critic worth his useless bachelor's degree knows that the filmmaker's intentions are not that important—and Lehmann's father, an honest-to-God, German-born Freudian psychoanalyst, would likely agree with me. Cinematographer Francis Kenny says in the *Heathers* DVD featurette "Swatch Dogs and Diet Coke Heads" that his original intention was to start the film "in a very safe, pastel tone, to try and get the audience to feel that they were going to watch a very bright comedy. And then suck them in, not just with the words but with the depth of color, and as the story turned darker, I would therefore start to go into a darker tone." Thankfully, this doesn't happen—the shoulder pads[8] take care of placing our film in the Reagan era without the addition of pastels, thank you. The consistent color saturation tells a more interesting story, I think.

At the fade-in, the Heathers and Veronica are introduced immediately with clothes that match their croquet balls and their personalities. The colors don't just pop, they pour off the screen. The blacks and blues of Veronica's outfits pierce us, remind us of her sadness, how masculine she appears next to her peers (the monocle, the relative smallness of her hair), and the walking bruise she is. Heather McNamara, the cowardly secretary of defense, is cloaked in yellow (and when forced to pick a pseudonym on the radio show *Hot Probs*, she chooses the flaxen cartoon hero Tweetie). She even tries to overdose on yellow pills. Heather Chandler's red, shoulder-padded jacket screams power the way James Dean's windbreaker does in *Rebel without a Cause*. Her lipstick is bright red; the inside of her locker is crimson. It has to be mentioned that Westerburg High School's colors are red and white, placing Kurt and Ram and their omnipresent letter jackets in the same rich, privileged camp as Chandler. Dennis the yearbook editor (Phill Lewis), who spreads the "Heather Chandler had warmth and her death is a great loss" meme through the school, shares her taste in couture: he wears a bright red sweater in his big scene. And there's the oft-discussed red scrunchie, over which the film's

---

[8] And, in all fairness, Daniel Waters freely admits that "the shoulder pads were already kind of dated at the time."

title is projected during the opening credits, and which is handed down like the Excalibur of popularity (J.D. takes it from the dead Heather Chandler and bestows it on Heather Duke, knowing full well she'll use it for evil) until it lands (justly?) in the hands and soot-blackened hair of Veronica. And—screw it—Heather Duke spends the movie jealous of Chandler's power (holding the talismanic scrunchie until Veronica takes it from her in the last scene), and she's dressed in green, the color of bile, the color of envy. She also switches over to red (after conquering her bulimia, a disorder marked by a lot of green) once Heather Chandler, her oppressor, is taken out of the picture. The red goes deep; Veronica tells us that Duke even performs Chandler's trademark cruel fake-mash-note prank on another nerd student, and she raids her red locker, taking a bunch of key rings that presumably hold the keys to the "kingdom."[9] The only time she returns to her previous green is when she dons a fatigue jacket (law-enforced stoner gear in the '80s) to get the burnouts to sign her "petition"—which of course turns out to be J.D.'s masterpiece, a massive suicide note

---

[9] We never see her use the keys, nor do we see her take any of the books in Chandler's locker, one of which is *The Castrated Family*, a 1977 book about what author Harold T. Voth refers to as "pathological parenting"— that is, parental behavior that results in maladjusted children. Voth warned of seismic cultural shifts and how they threatened the nuclear family. He was also on the governing board of NARTH, the National Association for Research and Therapy of Homosexuality, which works tirelessly to "cure" homosexuality. Are we to take this as a sign of Chandler's right-leaning politics?

covered with genuine signatures of kids who don't realize what they're signing.

The fashion blog Enjoy Your Style writes in sharp detail on the subject of color in the film, pointing out that Betty Finn and Martha Dumptruck are both introduced wearing pink, an inescapably weak color that puts them at the bottom of the school's social order. Enjoy Your Style also makes a great observation about an accessory: Heather McNamara gives Veronica Heather Chandler's old Swatch, the band of which is blue *and* red. This is Veronica, torn between her two allegiances: to herself, and to the social hierarchy she helps support (indeed, that she helped build, to continue the Albert Speer comparison). And every time she sees how much "time" she has left, she will see that conflict.

"Color me impressed," says J.D. toward the end of the film (and his life). Color us impressed, J.D.: You've just deliberately referenced a Paul Westerberg-penned Replacements song (off 1983's *Hootenany*) while simultaneously drawing our attention to the film's chief aesthetic appeal. *Heathers'* colors hum and vibrate and make the Hughes oeuvre look like dun public domain films from the 1930s. They echo the brilliant hues of Douglas Sirk's melodramas, with their heightened visuals and emotions. In fact, Lehmann speaks very fondly of being exposed to Sirk in his youth. As arch as *Heathers* can be, it's a very intense piece of work, filled with nervous laughter and horror, and colors that signify the melodrama—imagined and real—that is high school. High school is very funny, very cruel, very sad, very scary. Very . . . very.

Lehmann's youthful and magnificent obsession with Sirk makes *Heathers* the weird niece that lives in the attic in the house that's owned by *All That Heaven Allows*. I'll elaborate: The 1955 melodrama, set in a conservative Connecticut town, features a widowed Jane Wyman falling in love with her gardener, an insanely charismatic Rock Hudson. To see Hudson open a wine bottle with his teeth is to understand, finally, why our moms all died a little when his secret came out in the '80s. Hudson's character is quite a few years younger than Wyman's, and hardly in her social stratum, so the whole town seems to turn on her—the gossips, the country club, her hypocritical children. Wyman (the actress was newly divorced from Ronald Reagan, and wears her emotions on her sleeve) breaks your heart with every forlorn glance at her encroaching surroundings. When the film ends happily, it's earned. You've been through hell with the poor woman, and your joyful tears have not come cheap. Now, if all this camp and treacle sounds like the total antithesis of *Heathers*, remember: We're dealing with the bitterness of small-town judgment and the viral quality of gossip, and it's all being presented with meticulous *mise-en-scène* and eye-popping colors. In interviews, Sirk often referred to his "excessive" presentation of the material. And here's another Sirk quote that ties the two films together: "This is the dialectic—there is a very short distance between high art and trash, and trash that contains an element of craziness is by this very quality nearer to art."

Lehmann is just as guilty of excessive presentation. When asked if he regrets anything about his first feature, he points

out the self-conscious film student affectations that pop-up throughout—the low angle shots, the wide lenses—and recounts his insecurities ("Maybe I shouldn't go so low. Will it take people out of the movie?"). But in almost the same breath, Lehmann changes his tune: Maybe it takes a young director, he notes, to bring that "element of craziness." Lehmann has done great work in TV, helming shows like HBO's brilliant *The Comeback* and several episodes of the fun and pulpy *True Blood*. But his film work has diminished in excess, and he's paid a huge price for it, in terms of critical response. And maybe that craziness *is* what brings us closer to art, or at least to the art that other Sirk disciples (Rainer Werner Fassbinder, Todd Haynes, John Woo[10]) create. If we dismiss *All That Heaven Allows* as an over-the-top, proto-chick flick, we're missing out on a really gorgeous piece of

---

[10] Um, no, fuck *you*. *The Killer* is just *Magnificent Obsession* with kickass gunfights.

anti-'50s complacency propaganda, which was made smack dab in the *middle* of the 1950s. Similarly, if we shrug off *Heathers* as a cheap, cynical spoof on *Sixteen Candles* instead of appreciating its moody beauty, we rob ourselves of fully enjoying one of the great (indeed, few) satires of the 1980s.

A Stop at the Snappy Snack Shack

Michael Lehmann on the Look of Heathers

"I like the aesthetic of a low camera angle on a wide-angle lens, I think it's beautiful . . .

"First of all, I don't look at the world through a 50 millimeter lens, which is your standard lens, I never do, forget it. I see all of *that*"—gesturing broadly across the room—"and it's wide. And the distortion you get from a wide-angle lens doesn't feel like distortion. I used to draw cartoons as a kid, and I used to draw people with huge noses and I feel like—that's how people look, they sort of come at you that way.

"Directors of photography hate them, it's hard for them to light because they've got a ceiling, big ceiling in the background . . . everything becomes difficult. And wide lenses in general are hard to light for because there are fewer places to put the lights. And longer lenses are more flattering: they flatten facial features, they throw the background out of focus, and they're selective in what they see . . .

"The filmmakers I liked to watch when I was younger were Stanley Kubrick and Roman Polanski, and both of them, you know, favored low, wide angles a lot. So to me, that was good filmmaking. That was what the good filmmakers did.

"And also, at that time (the late 1980s), it was very fashionable to use long, long lenses. There was a style, sort of a Tony Scott style of movies that were more action driven or

beauty driven, where close-ups would be shot on a 200 millimeter lens and people would look gorgeous and they'd be backlit and the background would be way out of focus and it was . . . a real late-'80s, '90s style of filmmaking, that was dynamic in very different ways. I didn't like that. I was opposed to that.

"And I was also opposed to . . . I mean, I like John Hughes's movies because they were fun, but he always shot a very standard style, you know, what you'd call a more neutral style, and I didn't want to do that."

You Don't Deserve My Fucking Speech

The Dialogue of *Heathers*

My freshman-year dorm room was adorned with a few things: a Monty Python poster (Graham Chapman and Eric Idle crucified at the end of *Life of Brian*), a black and white Woody Allen picture, a few random fliers from rock shows I had seen that year, and my prized possession: the *Heathers* poster I had bought at Jerry Ohlinger's movie memorabilia shop on 14th street.[11] I'd be lying if I told you I didn't use it as an easy litmus test. The people I continued to hang out with throughout freshman year had seen the film and loved it. It was greeted that school year—1989–90—with either indifference or a serene nod and what amounts to great film criticism when you're eighteen: "Man, that movie has the best lines . . ."

One of the things that keeps *Heathers* from being just a sad little time capsule of the '80s is its inventive use of slang. As mentioned, I lived through high school in the '80s and can attest that at no point were things just "very," no one ever said "fuck me gently with a chainsaw," and no one was ever accused of having eaten "a brain tumor for breakfast." Waters eschews the actual awesome, fresh slang of the '80s to create a whole new, damn-near Burgessian parlance for his

---

[11] I paid twenty bucks for it. Ohlinger's has since moved uptown, and a *Heathers* poster (a folded one-sheet) will now run you a hundred and fifty.

high schoolers, maybe even as a nod to the Nadsat language of *A Clockwork Orange*. An early draft of the *Heathers* script contains the following exchange between Heather Chandler and her mother:

INT. Heather Chandler's Bedroom—Day

HEATHER CHANDLER's bedroom is lushly and expensively furnished with a glass coffee table as an eye-catching centerpiece.

HEATHER CHANDLER half-sleeps in twisted bedsheets as MRS. CHANDLER sticks her head in the door.

          MRS. CHANDLER
We are leaving soon for your grandmother's. If you care to join us . . .

          HEATHER CHANDLER
Bag that.

          MRS. CHANDLER
Is that a "No" in your lingo?

As the door closes, HEATHER CHANDLER raises her arm and gives her departed Mother "the finger."

          HEATHER CHANDLER
Lingo this.

The scene does not appear in the finished film, where the slang is mostly ersatz and is never addressed. This is just the way people talk in the alternate universe that is Sherwood, Ohio. It's another smack in the face of the Hughes films, which are pretty meticulous renderings of how people talked to each other at the time—and are as linguistically relevant now as the medieval morality plays. It's important to note that the one time authentic '80s jargon is used, it's by the priest at Heather Chandler's funeral. Glenn Shadix plays the kindly father, called Father Ripper in the film, Father Faust (!) in an earlier draft. From his eulogy: "We must pray the other teenagers of Sherwood, Ohio know the name of that 'righteous dude' who can solve their problems . . . It's Jesus Christ and he's in the book." "Righteous" and "dude" *were* part of teenspeak at the time, and had already been immortalized by another clueless adult, Grace, the Wite-Out sniffing secretary (Edie McClurg) speaking of the hero in *Ferris Bueller's Day Off*. But most of *Heathers* vernacular sprung fully-grown from Waters' mind. It's deliberately incongruous and never appropriate, which is why posterity has been kind to the big green eyes of Shannen Doherty as she inquires, "Why are you pulling my dick?"

Waters wisely gives a lot of his best lines to Veronica, who avoids the movie comedy pitfall of flavorlessly reacting to the craziness around her. "My teen angst bullshit has a body count!" "Swatch dogs and Diet Coke heads." "Suicide gave Heather depth, Kurt a soul, Ram a brain." The catch is that these *bon mots* are all written to *herself*. Veronica is protagonist and narrator of the film, and her journal is the recipient of her most insightful thoughts. Somewhere about two-thirds of the way into the film, she stops journaling, and it is then that she is able to break out of her complacency and proactively end the violence with one final burst of retributive violence. In this respect, she is a lot like Hamlet. Think of it: Any Shakespearean scholar will point out that Hamlet stops soliloquizing—stops talking to us, in effect—in Act IV, and that's when he is able to be at peace and avenge his father. As solipsistic as *Heathers* and all teen films can be, this one makes the point that all the journaling in the world won't save you when faced with real threats.

The Shakespearean connection does not end there. "I came from a point of Shakespeare, I guess," Waters says when asked about the film's "lingo":

> Shakespeare has a certain timelessness . . . I'm pretty sure people didn't speak like that even in the day, so . . . I took my cue from Shakespeare, in that "let's create our own language, and let's not worry about if this is the way people really talk," which is somehow always held up as what you should really strive for as a screenwriter. To a certain extent, yes, but . . . a lot of times if you do it half-real, half-florid it really comes off wrong. So I had to commit to a stylized language from the get go.

Waters further points out, "If you try to coddle to the culture that's happening right now . . . what you think is happening, what you think is hip . . . it's kind of the light of a star, from a planet that blew up 500 years ago." Which of course it is: even in 1985's *The Breakfast Club*, Judd Nelson's devastating putdown of Anthony Michael Hall ("neo-maxi-zoom-dweebie") drew a reaction teetering between embarrassed laughter and head scratching. It was already pretty dated, the term "dweeb" originating as early as 1968[12], when it was a variant of "feeb," or an acronym for either "dimwitted Eastern-educated bore," or, preferably, "dick with eyebrows." Maybe it sounded evergreen while it was being written.

The slang in *Heathers* is also notable in that it is spoken mostly by the girls. The jocks (and I'm adopting the film's archetypes here, with all due respect to high school athletes across the country) speak in grunts, the nerds stumble over the easiest sentences, and Jason notably rises above most of the slang. Oh, he has a way with words, sure, but things are not "very" and he does not ask about your "damage"[13] and he is not concerned with whether or not you are "pulling [his] dick." What are Waters and Lehmann—we'll call them the co-authors of the film—saying about the way men and women talk to each other? When the men talk to each other, it's clear-cut, harsh, and homophobic: "Doesn't this cafeteria have a no

---

[12] According to the Merriam Webster Collegiate Dictionary, but 1972 according to the Oxford English Dictionary. Chalk that up to the term originating in the States and taking a while to make it to the United Kingdom.

[13] Years later, on the "Return to Westerburg High" feature on the twentieth anniversary DVD, Waters cops to stealing the phrase "What's your damage?" from a camper back in his camp counseling days in Toronto. So, you know, technically, it is still not *American* slang.

fags policy?" "Answer him, dick." The aforementioned "That pudwapper just stepped on my foot!" Straightforward, heard it before, keep moving, not much to see here. But the viciousness of the way the women talk to each other makes you cringe. Even awkward exchanges that don't ring true—

HEATHER CHANDLER
You were nothing before you met me! You were playing Barbies with Betty Finn! I got you into a Remington Party! What's my thanks? It's on the hallway carpet. I got paid in puke!

VERONICA
Lick it up, baby. Lick. It. Up.

—are incredibly specific in their unpleasantness. Maybe we're not all that articulate in high school, but we can be pretty nasty. From an exchange with a dear friend in the eighth grade:

HER
At least my mom doesn't make me go to her office after school like I'm a toddler.

ME
At least my parents don't go to Europe and leave me behind.

Nowhere is there a zinger as succinct as "I got paid in puke," but there's a lot of sting in that absolutely true exchange. And the amazing thing? I'm still friends with that girl. The viciousness of school fades. We forgive, even if we don't forget. It is understood that in high school (in this case, junior high school) we are awful to each other, much more directly than we are as adults. And our verbiage was not catchy or poetic. When we did try to be hyper-articulate, we often fell tragically, comedically short. My friends and I tried our hand at our own slang, prior to and independent of *Heathers*. We'd been reading *Hamlet* in English class, and we were struck giggly by the term "spake" as the past tense of "speak." Sue us, we were sixteen and it sounded like "spunk." And so it began: when someone said something true, we started proclaiming "Matt just spake sooth." This evolved to "Spake it!" and then devolved to "When Matt said *Fletch Lives* sucked, he got spake all over me."

Waters's style—and make no mistake, he has one—fits satire very well. Its exaggerated rhythms and overwritten emotional histrionics fit in well with Joseph Heller, say, or Matt Groening. When he writes a conventional popcorn movie—*Hudson Hawk*, on which he shared writing credit—he falls into thorny territory. His second (and last) collaboration with Michael Lehmann, *Hawk* is a heist movie, an action comedy, an attempt at being one of the great '80s action comedies (which include *Midnight Run* and 50 percent of all Eddie Murphy movies), yet Bruce Willis's smirky delivery of Waters's dialogue makes the whole show seem a little arch, a little contrived, lacking the social heft of *Heathers* or even Waters's later screenplays, including the soon-to-be-discussed *Batman Returns*. *Hudson Hawk* is nowhere nearly as bad as you might've heard; that it beat the Vanilla Ice vehicle *Cool as Ice* and the Chevy Chase/Dan Akyroyd clusterfuck *Nothing but Trouble* for the Razzie that year is an O.J.-sized miscarriage of justice. Lehmann's big budget debut is slick and fast-paced, and my father went to his death defending the film[14]. But there's a reason I'm writing this book and not that one.

In a 2008 interview, Waters has a charmingly glass-half-full hindsight perspective on *Hawk*: "If any other writer woulda done it, it would have been a mediocre action movie that we would have completely forgotten. But it took me to make it the world's worst movie."

---

[14] No kidding. From his hospice bed, in a lucid moment between morphine administrations, my dad and I were having another movie talk and he said, "You know what's underrated? *Hudson Hawk*."

A Stop at the Snappy Snack Shack

An Email Interview with Heather #1

After we broke up, Heather #1 graduated and we didn't see each other for about a year. The smoke cleared—I started dating, so did she— and she got back in touch. We've been good friends ever since. She saw Heathers *on her own that spring and thought the same thing I did: It's John Bowie's story, since he dated two Heathers! Badumbump. She also pointed out something really interesting to me when we were dating: Charlie Brown's iconic and unobtainable Little Red-Haired Girl is also named Heather.*

Heather #1 lives in Brooklyn, almost has her Master's in children's literature, and has worked in children's publishing for the better part of a decade.

On her reaction to first seeing the film:

I'm sure this is only because it's my own name, but it's the name: both title and characters. "Heather" has always seemed to represent this all-American, sporty, smart, kind, milk-and-honey, Ivory soap girl (think Heathers Locklear, Thomas, and Graham), so to have a movie where this name represents girls who are anything but those positive things was jarring and refreshing. And frankly, made me feel better about having landed somewhere in the middle between the traditional Heathers and the filmed ones.

On her recollections of your author from high school:
Keeping in mind that we didn't meet until midway through
my senior year, my memories of you in high school are admittedly slim. After we met, I do remember moments in
class (that infamous "You really don't know what we're
doing here, do you, Mr. Bowie?"[15] jab in Latin, for example) . . . I remember wracking my brain at the time trying
to place you in a class: Where did we sit in relation to each
other? Had we ever been in a group conversation? Did
we have anyone in common? And I came up blank on all
counts. I'm not sure what that says about either of us. After
meeting, you became such an intense part of my life (however briefly) and the memories are a mixed bag, but mostly
because of my own issues. You were this wickedly smart,
funny guy who was so pop-culturally aware—I really felt
left in the dust (and I often still feel that way). But you also
came across as needy and sometimes insecure and trying so
intensely hard to build a relationship that there was a fragil-
ity that came through. There's no way I could have articu-
lated this back then, but I that's what I remember.

On her experiences in high school in general:
High school was a weird time for me. I'd come from suburban Seattle and still had very close ties there. Having grown
up all over the states, I really expected to have the typical
suburban high school experiences—and Humanities (and

---

[15] An accurate quote from our shared Latin teacher, Mr. Segall, with
whom I now have a cordial Facebook relationship. *Sic vita est.*

New York City overall) didn't allow for that. My friends in Seattle were living that all-American high school life, and I'd get reports from them, but there was a gulf between my New York City experiences and theirs. They were reporting on marching band, homecoming games, drivers' ed, pep rallies . . . and here I was at a school that was being run like a college, no band, no football, enjoying the freedom a subway token allowed, staying out half the night, cutting school to hang out at the Met . . .

One thing I did love about Humanities was that it was run like a college—that we had core classes and electives and that the electives were sometimes so off the wall. I also loved that there seemed to be several groups of cool kids. In the suburbs, I think everyone instantly turns to the jocks and cheerleaders, but for us, I think the swim team held as much social power as Fleisig's kids.[16]

On where your author would have fit into the film:
I don't think you are [represented]. I feel like there are groups in the film we don't see or get to know, and to get those groups you'd have to composite the characters we do see: you might have been a stoner/parking lot kid crossed with the geek table with a dash of Peter Dawson.

A fair assessment. I would probably add some Betty Finn to my cocktail, and maybe even some Martha Dumptruck. But we're still not quite close on why this film holds so much appeal for me. Heather

---

[16] A reference to the late drama teacher Mr. Alan Fleisig.

#1 *paints a very accurate picture of high school life in Manhattan's Chelsea neighborhood. A high school that couldn't look less like Westerburg High.*

A sad side note on Peter Dawson. In earlier drafts, he's a venal hypocrite who pockets people's charitable donations, and there's that aforementioned massive subplot (so massive that I might be misusing the term "subplot"; let's just call it Act Two), wherein he forms the Genesis Club to draw positive attention to the school after the media blitz surrounding Heather Chandler's apparent suicide. In an unsettling bit of irony, the actor playing Dawson, Jeremy Applegate—the man who utters the line "Dear Lord, please make sure this never happens to me because I don't think I could handle suicide"—took his own life in 2000.

Big Fun Are Tuneless Euro-Fags

The Music of *Heathers* and the Phenomenon of Teen Suicide

There isn't any music. Not in the way you'd expect there to be in a film of the 1980s, a pretty flawless decade for film soundtracks. Pick up the CD of *Fast Times at Ridgemont High* for a great, diverse data dump of what the decade sounded like (really diverse: there's Oingo Boingo, you'll find two ex-Eagles, a great Go-Go's B-side, and the one Jackson Browne song everyone can agree on liking). You're more of a new wave snob? Well, obviously you're gonna want the *Valley Girl* soundtrack, or *Pretty in Pink.* The soundtrack to *Heathers*, only recently made available on iTunes, is limited to David Newman's electronic score. Newman, son of famed Twentieth Century Fox composer Alfred Newman (*How The West Was Won, The Seven Year Itch*), was apparently *the* guy to score your medium-budget '80s comedy: He also provided music for *Bill & Ted's Excellent Adventure, Throw Momma from the Train*, and *The War of the Roses.* His extensive body of work continues to this day, but *Heathers* has a very specific sound. The artificial keyboards date the film, sure, but also provide the same kind of chill that can be found in John Carpenter's scores for his own *Halloween* or *Escape from New York*—notice how "J.D. Blows Up" echoes them.

There are three songs (actually, only two, but two versions of one of them) in the film, and they set a keen tone. It opens with a lush version of "Que Sera, Sera," a Doris Day staple rife with '50s *laissez faire* optimism. Though not initially recorded by her, Day made it famous by singing it in Alfred Hitchcock's *The Man Who Knew Too Much*. If you've seen the Hitchcock film, the song can spark some associative tension, and then there's just the delicious wit of starting this film, in all its violence and cynicism, with the decidedly inappropriate lyrics:

> *When I was just a little girl*
> *I asked my mother, what will I be?*
> *Will I be pretty, will I be rich?*
> *Here's what she said to me:*

> *Que sera, sera,*
> *Whatever will be, will be.*
> *The future's not ours to see.*
> *Que sera, sera,*
> *What will be, will be.*

Go ahead, Veronica, ask your mother what "will be." I doubt she'll be able to guess.

It's important to point out that it is *not* Doris Day's version of the song that opens the film; Day vetoed the use of her version due to the film's profanity. What replaces it is a *very* faithful cover by New York City-based alt-folkie Syd Straw. Straw has indie cred to burn (her first album features collaborations with a then-hip Michael Stipe and a young Matthew Sweet), so her cover doesn't need to strip the song down and tear it up. The strings are rich, she sings without winking, and most people think it actually is Doris on lead vocal. The film ends with the much more soulful version recorded in 1973 by Sly and the Family Stone.

Lehmann had considered using metal (which was going through a watershed phase at the time; bands like Metallica and Megadeth were finding both their artistic and commercial footing, while in the UK, Iron Maiden was dishing out terrifically pompous mini-operas like the concept album *Seventh Son of a Seventh Son*). An appealing idea on paper, certainly, and fitting with the anger at the core of the film. Plus, the eighties were filled with suicide pacts that were blamed on metal— watch the creepy documentary *Dream Deceivers* for a fascinating examination of Reno parents who try to blame Judas Priest for their (abused) children's suicides. But metal doesn't leave a lot of room for subtlety or wit, and Lehmann points out that it would have grinded against the film's dreamy aesthetic. A classical score was discussed, obviously, by the two Kubrick nerds Lehmann and Waters. Also nixed. As a temp soundtrack, Art of Noise was used—interesting for a number of reasons. They fit the dream-like atmosphere, and if memory serves, my girlfriend Heather #2 used to listen to them as she was falling asleep. But the conventional route of peppering the film with contemporary pop hits never gained any traction, due to Lehmann's fears it would date the film as badly as current slang. The two versions of "Que Sera, Sera" (recorded sixteen years apart) float in and out of the film, never nailing down a diegetic time. The Syd Straw version was recorded in the '80s, but sounds like it's from the '50s, and the Sly and the Family Stone take, recorded in 1973, adds an element of soul that seems incongruous swelling up over the visual—a bloodied Veronica walking down the hallway as a wheelchair-bound Martha Dumptruck does donuts around her. The songs don't really fit, and that might be the point. "Whatever will be" turns out to be an unlikely pairing of people who are sitting out prom night and maybe, just maybe, starting a new social order in the process. *That's* what will be.

The film wasn't always going to take place in this music-free alternate universe; there are some misguided music references in earlier drafts, like the following exchange at the Remington College party:

> BRAD
> So what do you say we head up to my room and have a real party. I've got the best Windham Hill CD collection in the dorm.

And later:

> BRAD
> Excellent. Veronica, ever do *cocaine*?

> VERONICA
> Ever since Phil Collins did that MTV anti-drug commercial, I refuse everything.

Now, in 1989, Windham Hill connoted a very specific personality type: a faux-sensitive, New Age, aspiring-yuppie who liked his music cranked up to three on some cherry Aiwa speakers and really "got" what Mannheim Steamroller was trying to do. However, Windham Hill was bought out by Sony in the mid-'90s (like Aiwa, as it turns out) and has not had a web presence since 2007. Obviously, the Windham Hill joke makes me laugh, but I can't imagine too many people younger than me enjoying it.

And then there's Kurt Kelly's drunken, fruitless come-on to Veronica in the pasture—a wonderful, deep focus shot. In the foreground, Veronica comes up the hill toward the camera. Middle ground: There's Kurt trying to get over the fence, way too drunk to do so. Background? Ram, in no uncertain terms, date-raping Heather McNamara. The sole musical accompaniment to this scene is Kurt's fucked-up warbling of Marvin Gaye's semi-contemporary "Sexual Healing." It's only two lines, we never hear the actual song, and the scene is such a perfect vignette of the worst rural high school date ever that we can hardly begrudge this one reference to the music of the '80s. Besides, Waters is quick to point out, "There's an instinct that Michael and I have, we will interrupt the integrity of the movie to go for the silly laugh."

The other song in *Heathers*, of course, is the fictional Big Fun[17] hit "Teenage Suicide (Don't Do It)." Edits for budget or time somehow prevented the Big Fun video (a huge part

---

[17] Not to be confused with the real Big Fun, a UK boy band trio who had a string of European hits starting in 1989 (the year *Heathers* was released). Looking, well, a lot like the duo Wham!, Big Fun released pablum-like "Can't Shake the Feeling" on a willing British audience before disbanding in 1994.

of early drafts) from being shot, but it was meant to be pretty much as you've imagined it. From Waters first draft:

> *Two overgorgeous young men wearing TRENDY HAIR, and TRENDY CLOTHES stand before all white background and shout/sing directly to the viewer. They are much like the duo Wham!*

The lyrics to the hit, in this first draft:

> *Times are mean for a teen—we know!*
> *Parents ignore, teachers bore—we know!*
> *But there is more than one way to go!*
> *Teenage suicide—don't do it.*

And so on, in that fashion. The song is kind of brilliant in its inanity, cashing in on a serious problem and offering the worst kind of Reagan-era "this is harmful, avoid it" treacle as a solution. The song's banal lyrics somehow get funnier when you realize how dire the situation had become by the late '80s. According to the Child Welfare League of America, between 1952 and 1995, the teen suicide rate *tripled* in the United States (it has hovered at around 12 percent of all teen fatalities since). And it's important to note that a 1997 study by the Youth Risk Behavior Surveillance System revealed that 27.1 percent of females seriously considered suicide, compared to 15.1 percent of males (another reason why the film is so female-centric). The reasons for these terrifying statistics are sprawling, way too big to go into here, but you can take economic status, ethnicity (the problem is so much bigger among native populations, and less of an issue among African Americans), mental health, and dozens of other variables into account. And to this serious scourge, Big Fun offer:

> *Razor blades and cyanide, why try it?*
> *Off a jagged cliff, in a raging tide,*
> *Why try it?*

What's being satirized here is not teen suicide, but the glib, reductive reactions to an incredibly complex problem. What's being satirized is Nancy Reagan's foolish and ineffective anti-drug campaign, and the people who tell visibly depressed teens to "cheer up." I bristle whenever people suggest the film is pro-suicide, and I laugh with Daniel Waters when he jokes, "Pro-suicide? If anything, it's pro-homicide!" By this, he means that there's really only one suicide in the film, and it's the suicide of a homicidal maniac. Who has just killed a lot of really unlikable people. But what *I* mean by "pro-homicide" is something more along the lines of, "Sometimes I'd like to kill the dipshits who romanticize suicide, and the sanctimonious nitwits who blithely advise against it."

Waters has strong words for the attention that suicide is given by the media, and likens it to the credence they give the school shootings that have cropped up in recent years. "The way the media acted—you know, 'This is now on the menu,'" he says, is similar to "the line in *Heathers*: 'Whether to commit suicide or not is the most important decision a teenager has to make.'" He elaborates, taking on the condescending tone of an ineffectual guidance counselor: "'You're feeling depressed, so, you know, we really recommend you don't kill ten people at your school . . .' This is not the way to talk about this!" In his book *Suicide and Homicide Among Adolescents*, Paul C. Holinger even concedes that "this increase in the scientific literature on youth suicide has corresponded to a steady increase in adolescent suicide rates." One wonders if teen suicide might be the one awful thing that might actually go away if we would just stop talking about it quite so much.

Suicides often come in clusters, whether we do anything about them or not. Bergen County, New Jersey saw a spate in the years 1986 and 1987 (while *Heathers* was being written, or at least revised), including a pretty famous case that I remember in which four teens gassed themselves in a garage adjacent to an empty house. Their deaths had been triggered by the "alcohol-related deaths" of their friends, all of which had the earmarks of suicide: depressed teens walking into ponds or oncoming trains. The quadruple suicide also led to copycat deaths, two in the same county within the next month. In a contemporary article, *Time* magazine quoted the then-president of the National Committee for the Prevention of Youth Suicide: "Kids see that this is a glamorous way to die, a way to get a lot of attention that they couldn't get in life . . . They see a kid that is a nonentity suddenly get attention, and that is what they have been struggling for."

And in the wake of this deeply upsetting crisis, here comes "Teenage Suicide (Don't Do It)," written by North Carolina musician Don Dixon. Dixon, like Straw, had worked with Michael Stipe. He co-produced REM's debut, *Murmur*, and a host of other jangly '80s bands, including the Smithereens and Guadalcanal Diary. Gone is the organic sound of those bands, replaced with a saccharine bounciness that is so unutterably lame that comparing it to Wham! is being unduly harsh to George Michael and Andrew Ridgeley. The drums are unmistakably fake. The keyboards, which are kind of haunting in Newman's score, here come off as just shrill. The lyrics are only slightly improved from Waters' draft:

> *My future looks dark 'cause my lights are out.*
> *Please pull this gun out of my mouth.*

Its only hook is its melodic sliding upward on the word "suiciiiiiiiiiiiiiiiiiiide." It's one of the most deliberately terrible songs ever written for a film (and I'm taking into account the actually quite catchy Spinal Tap numbers). It is not available on the soundtrack, but can be found on Dixon's solo record *(If) I'm a Ham, Well You're a Sausage*. I found a used copy on Amazon for four dollars.

A Statistic in *US-Fucking-A Today*

A Quick Word on the Incident at Columbine High School

A teen suicide is followed by endless exegesis. Dave Cullen's exhaustive book *Columbine* hit shelves ten whole years after the massacre that ended with the two assailants' suicides. Every influence, every utterance, every article of clothing is picked apart in a typically hopeless quest for the trigger. *What set this kid off? How did this happen? What did we, as a society, do wrong?*

Cullen's book is a compelling read, and it's not for me to say if it will help stave off another similar incident, but I'm put off by the lengthy chapters on Eric Harris and Dylan Klebold. The music they listened to, the books they read, the TV programs they watched are all analyzed, as are extensive chunks of their diaries and video journals. These are deep character studies, and by book's end you have the queasy feeling of having spent a lot of time in their rooms with them. It's time that would have been better spent before they died and took thirteen innocent people with them, and it's exactly the kind of attention that they wanted. The only catch is that they're not around to bathe in it.

One of the most chilling parts of the book is the discovery that they wanted to top the casualties of the Oklahoma City bombing. Not because they idolized Timothy McVeigh, or were as overtly racist as he was, or any of the idle conspiracy theories that popped up. They just wanted to exceed

McVeigh in carnage. That's all. No politics, no social critique. Just excess. In his journal, Harris makes repeated references to the "audience" of the impending massacre. And the investigation, the head scratching, the vague timelines and charts in *USA Today*, even the universal enmity, is just what a narcissistic teen wants. And a lot of teens, suicidal or not, are really narcissistic.

J.D. fits Cullen's profile of a psychopath. He, like Harris, is filled with a deep contempt for the people around him. J.D. treats his peers like the paper dolls he keeps on his bookshelf (right on top of the '70s puberty guide *Making Sense Out of Sex: A New Look at Being a Man*). He is charming and deceitful ("Ich lüge"), and despite getting suspended for wielding a gun in a cafeteria, no one suspects him for the genuine threat he is. He is also not the hero of the piece. Veronica is. He is a joke and a fraud, a wobbly James Dean wannabe who, like Eric Harris, makes a bomb that doesn't quite work (J.D. has to smack the faulty timer to get it running again). Harris's father was in the army, and the young man had been uprooted several times before settling in Littleton, and J.D.'s father drags him across the country, from convenience store town to convenience store town.

Harris was unusual among psychopaths in that he didn't start by unleashing his violent tendencies on animals. The one time we see J.D's room, we make out that he keeps an empty rodent cage in there—either the rodent is being mourned with an altar (his "room" left intact), or J.D. has done something to the rodent. Or both. J.D. also has no plans to commit suicide; Harris and Klebold always expected to die, but they expected it to be at the hands of the police. When J.D. breaks into Veronica's room, planning to win her back or else to kill her, he finds her already "dead"—having faked her death in order to protect herself. In an admittedly hackneyed chunk of exposition, J.D. reveals to her apparently lifeless body his plan to blow up the school in the biggest staged suicide yet. He then fondly wishes that he and Veronica could have "toasted marshmallows together" in the school's flaming ruins. J.D. is not intending to go out in a blaze of glory. His mission is to kill all his "inferiors"; in this regard, he is more of a textbook psychopath than Harris. Yet his last moment onscreen has him mimicking a Christ pose just before the dynamite strapped to his chest goes off. Unable to make a statement, unable to "scare people into not being assholes," he dies, a martyr for a lost cause. But he's already been shot, probably fatally, by a gun that he left in Veronica's room, thinking she was dead. So the question remains: Has he always expected to die? And if so, what for? Because he was alone in a world he hated? Because he, like Harris, thought he was God and despised everything around him? What works about the film now is that J.D. is refuted by Veronica, and that all of it is made so broad, so ridiculous, that I have trouble believing that any sane person who sees the movie could seriously consider shooting up his or her school. For what? So people you didn't like can lionize themselves on the local news?

Veronica, in her dream sequence, spits at her by-then-ex-boyfriend, "You're not a rebel, you're fucking psychotic." J.D. breezily replies, "You say tomayto, I say tomahto." To J.D., they're synonymous. And there's the creepy part—of *Heathers*, of the Columbine massacre, of every school shooting and disgruntled postal worker explosion. There are very, very sick, people in this world, and some of them just think that they're badasses.

On April 20, 1999, Waters was in a meeting with his old producer Denise DiNovi when the news came over CNN that there was some sort of siege going on in Littleton, Colorado. There had been a rash of smaller school shootings over the past year, so Waters was as concerned as anyone that it was reaching epidemic proportions, but didn't connect it to his work. Until he found out that the shooters were wearing trench coats, much like Jason Dean. Waters and Lehmann both braced themselves for an onslaught of media attention . . . which never really came. There had been a more aggressive dream sequence in the execrable *Basketball Diaries* from 1995, wherein Leonardo DiCaprio pulls out a shotgun in his New York City parochial school and starts laying waste to classmates and teachers (and just for the record, as of this writing, due to metal detectors, shit like that doesn't really happen in New York City schools). Lehmann, in an interview with *V Magazine*, said:

> I got really worried the day of Columbine. I had three or four messages on my machine—one from the *New York Times*, one from *Time* magazine—asking me to comment. That freaked me out because I don't want to comment on Columbine. I don't know anything about what led to it, and what a horrible idea to think that this movie made many years before had

contributed to these kids shooting a bunch of people in their school. Certainly it made me think. But then I also went and did a little research to find out if any of these kids made any *Heathers* references. Apparently, there were none. That wasn't part of their vocabulary. They were enamored of Leonardo DiCaprio in the *Basketball Diaries*. But there were enough similarities to spook me.

There are similarities, sure, and the kids, like all high school children, saw a lot of violent movies. Dylan Klebold wore a t-shirt showing Harvey Keitel from *Reservoir Dogs* in a yearbook photo, and he and Harris gave the day of their massacre the code name NBK, for *Natural Born Killers*. And despite all of that, who gives a shit, Tarantino is not in an actionable position. I saw the nauseating *Cannibal Holocaust* in high school and it didn't make me want to kill South Americans because, aside from some garden-variety depression, I'm not actually crazy. The film *Scream*, with its violent, hyper-articulate teenagers, owes a great debt to *Heathers*, and contains what I hoped would be the last word on this subject. Heroine Sidney (Neve Campbell) discovers the killers' identity and confronts them with the line, "You sick fucks have seen too many movies." And one of the killers responds, "Now, Sid, don't go blaming movies. Movies don't make psychos, they just make psychos more creative."

None of this stops anybody from looking into people's media consumption for clues after a tragedy. So it all rings very true when J.D. ingeniously plants a "meaningfully highlighted" copy of *Moby-Dick* in Heather Duke's room (during Veronica's dream sequence). We've seen Heather reading the book before—it's probably been assigned in class—and it's an onerous tome, certainly. The one word highlighted? "Eskimo" (which is actually spelled "eskimaux" in Melville's book). Reading the word at Heather Duke's dream funeral, Father Ripper bemoans the loss of a girl who felt as if she was on the isolated tundra. Of course, "eskimo" means nothing; it's a red herring planted by J.D. But after something like this, after a tragic loss of life, we feel the need to ascribe meaning, significance, to everything.

The original draft of the script uses *Catcher in the Rye* as Heather's last testament, but J.D. Salinger balked at the idea. It's almost too easy, *Catcher*, with its indictments of "phonies" and its ending set in some sort of mental health facility. *Moby-Dick* means less in the grand "teen-alienation" picture, so using it as the big clue is even more absurd. When you finish Cullen's Columbine book, you realize that the massacre was about nothing but two genuinely crazy kids—not Goth music, not gun legalization, and not bullying. Just two sick children who did everything wrong in their otherwise normal quest for attention.

Heathers came four short years after a highly rated TV movie called *Surviving*, which deals with the aftermath of a double teen suicide (perpetrated by Molly Ringwald and Zach Galligan). The parents are left to pick through the debris, and there's something very exciting about that; anyone who's ever considered suicide has probably had that flash of "everyone will be sorry, and they won't realize how much they love me until I'm gone." And the '80s saw a flurry of headlines, movies, and after school specials that dealt not so much with the gritty horror of suicide as much as with its aftermath.

The postmortem *A Desperate Exit* stars Malcolm-Jamal Warner, whose life is recalled in flashback after he inexplicably kills himself. Made in 1986, this after school special is a lurid mystery in the guise of a cautionary tale, its good intentions undercut by a ridiculous plot twist (the budding writer was wracked with guilt because he didn't stop another suicide! Depression had nothing to do with it!). The Keanu Reeves movie *Permanent Record* is all about the aftershocks of a young musician's suicide, and Reeves is left to contemplate the picturesque cliff where his friend ended his life. And it's before Reeves could act. *Dead Poets Society* came out a couple months after *Heathers* but is one of the worst offenders: Misunderstood by his parents (but loved by everyone else), budding actor Robert Sean Leonard has no choice but to end it all with his father's gun. Following the death, everyone, even his teacher—Robin Williams!— weeps, and we are meant to realize what a gentle soul we had in the departed. Who wouldn't want that send-off? Maybe we've even felt a pang of jealousy over a dead person's sudden spike in notoriety, deserved or not. Veronica points out that "suicide gave Heather depth, Kurt a soul, Ram a brain." And the media loves the image of artists who are too sensitive to deal with the world around them. The film skewers that phenomenon, but also points out how teenagers go absolutely apeshit around death.

In my interview with Heather #1, she alluded briefly to a Mr. Fleisig, our drama teacher at Humanities. He went on medical leave my senior year, and shortly after the school year started, it came down the wire that he had died of cancer (everyone read between the lines, and as was suspected, he had died of AIDS-related Kaposi's Sarcoma). There was a certain class of indoor-scarf-wearing drama kid who took the news badly, and I did, too. He'd been a fascinating guy. Like most drama teachers, he also taught English, and I read *Hamlet*, *A Separate Peace*, and *Siddhartha* in his class (an alienated teen triumvirate if ever there was one). So it sent shockwaves through the school, of course, especially with the added politicization of a death from AIDS. When drama students lose someone they love, you can only imagine the "I can't go on, yet I must go on" histrionics that take over. People sat in the auditorium, crying over old yearbooks. I wrote a brief but maudlin dedication to him for that spring's Play Program. But what struck me, and still does, was the way a lot of kids who never had his class, weren't in any of his plays, never knew the guy, jumped on the grief bandwagon. We had no suicides at my high school, but this death showed me that everyone in high school enjoys a good fad. Mourning was that year's side ponytail, or tapered jeans.

Why Are You Pulling My Dick?

Heathers as Social Satire

If the film works as satire at all, it's due to its reliance upon and then its subversion of the huge archetypes of high school (and by extension, the world). The girls are the meanest, the guys are the dumbest, and the teachers are so petty that they seem to be the juveniles, becoming more and more peripheral as the film moves on. It's as ridiculous as the famous satire *A Modest Proposal*, in which Jonathan Swift suggests the best way to cure Irish poverty is for the Irish to eat their own children. How better to combat high school classism than to kill the upper classes? Maybe that's an even more modest proposal . . .

Waters has a great quote about Westerburg High's hegemony: "The high school power center is female. At that age, boys are checkers and girls are chess." To elaborate: Veronica is chess, negotiating high school through communication, strategy, and occasional diversionary tactics (her straight-faced participation in Heather Chandler's memorial service, for example). She compromises constantly, agreeing to the Remington Party, the double date with Kurt, and eventually the double murder of Kurt and Ram. Chess is a more complicated game. Maybe you sacrifice a pawn to get a king.

The male characters are simpler—less sophisticated and ultimately less powerful. Anyone who is a parent to both a boy and a girl (as I am) will corroborate this: Boys are aggressive—their strength is physical—whereas girls become verbal at a much earlier stage. Kurt and Ram are pushy and bullying, but they're not really calling the shots. J.D. is very much checkers: "This is in my way. I will jump it." He is smarter than, but as aggressive as, Kurt and Ram. And they are in his way, literally cornering him in their first meeting in the cafeteria. His one attempt at psychological manipulation—getting Heather Duke to distribute his "petition" by threatening to make public childhood pictures of her socializing with Martha Dumptruck—is really just a way to cover up the biggest checkers move of all: blowing up a school with Norwegian dynamite.[18] It's also telling that Waters regrets this scene more than anything in the film, finding J.D.'s blackmail of Heather Duke a little too facile. Waters wishes that Jason had been a little more "Machiavellian" in his technique, that he had played up the vacuum of leadership in the school after Heather Chandler's death. And yet, if one could go back in time and "correct" that one scene, Jason might have been given more depth and nuance than he perhaps deserves. The blackmail is vulgar, simple, and stunningly effective. It is, in short, a checkers move. You probably could not make a comedy called *Jasons*, since it would just look like a first-person shooter video game—*Call of Duty* set in a high school. We're given a cursory explanation for Jason's

---

[18] Big Bud Dean speaks of "putting a Norwegian" in the basement of a Landmark hotel, probably a reference to DynoNobel, the company that Alfred Nobel started in Norway, which, to this day, makes most of the world's dynamite.

psychosis: His dad's crazy, his dad is indirectly responsible for his mom's death, and he's moved around so much that he's never been attached to anything. It's really a horrible, sad story and as such, Jason does not make this film a comedy. The film's humor comes from the verbal sparring, the equivocation, the vicious insults. It comes from people trying to build themselves up and curry favor by feigning compassion. The violence is shocking, and the sheer *wtf* nature of the first cafeteria shooting always makes me laugh, but it's not what we've signed on for.

The film is named after the female characters for a reason. Now, having said that, it would be extremely easy to dismiss Waters and Lehmann as misogynists, if you're the sort of freshman soc major who wants to see misogyny in everything. But while you might realistically be able to charge them with a certain degree of misanthropy in general, a particular hatred of women is far too simplistic an accusation. Yes, the women (actually girls) are horrible to each other. But has the world not forced this mutual abuse on them? Are they not aping the men in power in the adult world? And isn't that why, when faced with dissent, Heather Duke calmly and confusedly asks, "Why are you pulling my dick?" Where to start with that line? Obviously, she's trying to establish her masculinity, her alpha-male status at Westerburg. But her power does not come from having a dick, even a metaphorical one. It comes from skillful chess moves, from strategy, from having something for everyone; it comes from her ability to pull off an old military jacket to talk to the potheads. She struggles with her femininity as much as everyone in the film does. Heather

Chandler "rules the school," but among adults, at a college party, she is all but forced into a sex act that fills her with self-loathing. These women are trying to ape the checkers of men (right down to their shoulder pads which ape the carriage of the football team), and that's the problem.

The monocle that Veronica wears gives us a telling peek into her character and her melee with gender identity. A single corrective lens hanging from a chain was tradition-ally worn by men in the 1800s. This and her blue bathrobe give her a masculine quality that grows stronger once she stops journaling. Which coincides with her becoming more checkers ("You know what I need? Cool guys like you out of my life." *Bang!* This obstructs me, ergo it must go away now). The monocle also corrects the vision of only one eye—it, like all of *Heathers*, doesn't give you the whole picture.

The tragic part of the film is that for all the "feminine" strategy, manipulation, and subterfuge, it's the big, dumb, phallus gun that saves the day and the school. Veronica stops her introspection and kills J.D., one final murder that redeems her by preventing him from throwing the baby out with the bathwater and killing *everyone*, regardless of their guilt.

Waters continued to tweak convention and correctness after *Heathers*. As a hot young screenwriter, he came into some weird assignments. His follow up to *Heathers* was the Andrew Dice Clay vehicle *The Adventures of Ford Fairlane*. Waters had been taken to see the Diceman in a small comedy club as the comedian's star was rising and found him, maybe naively, to be a "brilliant parody of the male psyche." As Clay's concerts grew in size, so did his ego, and by the time the cameras rolled—with non-comedy director Renny Harlin at the helm—the film had gone through a lot of script changes that Waters had not approved and that slipped through his fingers. The result is a basically fun idea (a detective who exclusively solves rock'n'roll-themed crimes) sullied by Clay's gay-baiting machismo. Find the script online; there are some good moments.

Despite a critical drubbing, Waters still had a fan in Tim Burton, whose production company was headed by *Heathers* producer Denise DiNovi. This confluence led to his assignment to write the script for the second (and Burton's last) *Batman* film. 1992's *Batman Returns* stars Michael Keaton in his last round in the title role and Michele Pfeiffer as Selina Kyle . . . and her more famous alter-ego, Catwoman.

The comic book Catwoman made her first appearance in the first solo issue *Batman #1* as an unnamed cat burglar in a slinky suit, presented by creator Bob Kane as a romantic and criminal foil for the Caped Crusader. She's been given a bunch of origin stories: A former stewardess, she turned to crime after surviving a plane crash. Or she fled an abusive marriage and resorted to burglary after her husband stowed her family jewels away in a safe. Or she was a former prostitute who killed an abusive pimp (!). Writer Mindy Newell created an origin story wherein a thirteen-year-old Kyle discovers that the hall administrator at her orphanage is embezzling money, and she is swiftly punished for her knowledge: Like an unwanted cat, she is put into a bag and thrown into a river. She escapes, blackmails the administrator, and embarks on a life of crime. It is to this origin that Waters hews closest in his *Batman Returns* screenplay. Kyle is a timid secretary who discovers that her boss (Waters names the character Max Shreck) is working on a power plant that will drain Gotham City of energy. For her trouble she is thrown out a window, and mysteriously revived by cats. Yes, she's an administrative assistant; Waters omits the stuff about Selina being a child prostitute. He also places the blame for her conversion on a society that treats women so poorly:

> CATWOMAN
> The world tells boys to conquer the world, and girls to wear clean panties. A man dressed as a bat is a he-man, but a woman dressed as a cat is a she-devil. I'm just living down to my expectations. Life's a bitch—now so am I.

It's a very sympathetic portrayal of a *Batman* villain, and Pfeiffer brings a slinky humanity to the role. She even appropriates Helen Reddy's '70s feminist anthem: "I am Catwoman, hear me roar."

Heather Chandler has learned this same lesson without being thrown out of a window. A wonderfully telling scene from earlier drafts illustrates this paradox, the clean-pantied alpha girl's lament:

> VERONICA and HEATHER CHANDLER set themselves down with BETTY FINN and her LOOK-ALIKE FRIENDS.
>
> HEATHER CHANDLER (V.O.)
> Look at me. I look great. I'm the girl in the commercials and the videos.
>
> JOCKS' TABLE
>
> VERONICA and HEATHER CHANDLER warily stand at the outskirts of the JOCKS' bastion of vulgarity.
>
> HEATHER CHANDLER (V.O.)
> I'm the blonde in the bikini on the horse holding a Pepsi can.
>
> INT. STONERS' HALLWAY—DAY
>
> In a dark, smoky hallway, VERONICA and HEATHER CHANDLER cough toward a batch of STONERS in tattered forms of dress.

> HEATHER CHANDLER (V.O.)
> I'm the princess being spanked on the throne
> by Billy Idol's guitarist's guitar.

INT. THE FOODLESS FUND STAND—DAY

VERONICA and HEATHER CHANDLER accost PETER DAWSON at the Foodless Fund stand.

> HEATHER CHANDLER (V.O.)
> What do I get out of being friends with losers?
> I give them a piece of a winner and they stain
> me with loserness.

Note the sadomasochistic imagery here: Even the beauty gets punished by the beast (Billy Idol). If we expect women to be pristine and perfect, how can they not snap? Or at the very least, how can they not exert that pressure on the people around them? And if we can't take it, if we buckle under the pressure like Veronica or, worse, Betty Finn, if we, simply put, can only lose, can we fault Heather (or Catwoman) for trying to win?

It's these paradoxes that help the film succeed as a satire. Take the exchange between J.D. and his father: J.D. and Veronica are sitting on the couch, watching TV (the script has them watching *The Brady Bunch*; the film has them watching news coverage of Heather Chandler's death). Big Bud Dean enters and is greeted by his son with, "Why son, I didn't hear you come in." Big Bud replies, "Hey, Dad, how was work today?"

They continue in this fashion, Big Bud revealing all sorts of unsavory facts about his line of work—he blows up landmarks for new developments, etc.—and the exchange ends with:

> J.D.
>
> Jason, why don't you ask your little friend to stay for dinner?

> VERONICA
> (*awkwardly standing*)
>
> My mom's making my favorite meal tonight. Spaghetti. Lots of oregano.

> J.D.
>
> Nice. The last time I saw my mom, she was waving out the window of a library in Texas. Right, *Dad?*

BIG BUD DEAN stops rowing to grin a You-Think-You're-Tougher-Than-Me-But-You're-Not smile to J.D.

> BIG BUD DEAD [sic]
>
> Right, *son.*

Couple things. That pre-final draft typo is pretty fascinating. The "d" is actually not that close to the "n" on the keypad, and while I really try not to accuse people of Freudian slips too often, "Big Bud Dead" might have to be an exception. It reeks of the author's deep-seated aversion to authority.

But the larger issue is the pure satire at work here; Gilbert and Sullivan might have loved the topsy-turveydom of this running gag. With one notable exception, the kids are smarter than the adults (or at the very least, Veronica and J.D. are smarter than everyone else), and this is embodied in the clear linguistic role reversal of J.D. and Big Bud Dead's [sic] relationship.

And then, all of a sudden, J.D. drops the bit to show real vulnerability. He is a son who lost his mother. It might be the only time we see him as a human being. It might be the only time that Waters and Lehmann sell out a joke to show some integrity. When last we hear from Jason's dad, he's continuing the role reversal charade, trying to get his son's attention while Jason constructs one of his bombs. The last time we see guidance counselor Pauline Fleming (performed flawlessly by Penelope Milford), she is unloading her final bit of pre-fab wisdom on Veronica—the previously quoted "Whether to kill yourself is one of the most important decisions a teenager has to make"—and Veronica replies, "Get a job." To the guidance counselor. Whose job it is to make sure her students can find jobs.

All of this role reversal—and role questioning—leads us to *the line*. The line that, just once, makes the adults smarter than the kids. The line that gets repeated so often that we stop wondering if it's true and just click our tongues and accept it as part of who we are, our sad destiny.

Veronica can't believe how irrational her school is acting following the deaths of Kurt and Ram, and she explodes at her parents, "All we want is to be treated like human beings!" And her mom, in her sole moment of cogent clarity, shoots back:

Treated like human beings? Is that what you said, little Miss Voice of a Generation? Just how do you think adults act with other adults? You think it's all just a game of doubles tennis? When teenagers complain that they want to be treated like human beings, it's usually because they *are* being treated like human beings.

It's the moment in a *Heathers* screening where everyone gets a little quiet and pensive. Where the movie stops reveling in shock value and kicking sand in the face of pussy John Hughes movies and makes its point. The point isn't that kids are killing each other in this movie, or that the adults "don't get it," but it's far more disturbing: It's that people kill each other all the time in real life, and that the bonds of empathy are troublingly thin. The line flew over my head at the time, but every time I get that familiar sting from not being invited to a party, or slighted by gossip (and I'm in my very late thirties at this writing), that line rings in my head like a horrible gong. Do we ever graduate? Do we ever pass? Waters is proud of the line, sure, but he knows it can be used as a cop-out: If high school never ends, we're free to be two-faced, shameless dicks to each other forever. He points out that "the adage 'real life is like high school' has become so ingrained that it's kind of given people a pass." Waters points out that "there are not a lot of great college movies" because the raw emotions are starting to be either repressed or controlled, depending on your worldview. He believes "college was invented to keep eighteen- to twenty-two-year-olds off the street." So this viciousness might not be overt, but it's there: Witness the snarky comment about certified adult Tom Tancredo at the beginning of the book.

So it is this line—and its downright elegiac delivery by actress Jennifer Rhodes—that keeps me coming back to the film. *Heathers* works as a satire by using the high-school-as-society trope (maybe even creating it) and following it through to its logical conclusion . . . or falling just short. Maybe the school *should* blow up at the end. Maybe the school should self-destruct because the school is "society." Or maybe, maybe, it should end on a hopeful note. When J.D., bloodied and bruised and missing his middle finger (Veronica having just shot it off) declares, "Let's face it, the only place different social types can genuinely get along with each other is in heaven," it's clearly a line left over from the earlier "prom in heaven" draft. Yet Lehmann has slyly intercut the fight scene between Veronica and J.D. with scenes from the pep rally going on just above the boiler room in the school's gymnasium. The effect? Sure, we're building suspense in a John Frankenheimer way (the DVD director commentary tips the hat to *Black Sunday*), but there's something else going on. Everyone gets a close-up: Rodney, Betty Finn, Peter Dawson (with a heretofore unseen girlfriend), Heather Duke. All of them together, all of them enjoying themselves as they cheer on the Westerburg Rottweillers. Maybe J.D.'s way isn't the way, as appealing as it might initially seem. After all, society has survived, against all odds, since Mesopotamia in, what, 5000 BC? There are existential threats that come along every couple of decades, but they're inevitably followed by heroes

rising to cool things off, to steer mankind away from anni-
hilation and restore peace and order. We can only hope that
a real leader will step up, grab the scrunchie, and use it for
the greater good. Hitler threatened Churchill, and Churchill
prevailed. Then Churchill threatened Gandhi, and Gandhi
prevailed. Veronica threatened high school, but when J.D.
threatened Veronica, she saved high school. If you wonder
why I've just placed Ryder's character among such hallowed
political company, you need only ask yourself if there's any institution in the world more petty and venal than an American
high school. (A hint: it's obliquely referred to in the introduc-
tion to this very book.) In an email, Waters elaborates very
briefly on his short-lived plan for a sequel:

> Very softly spitballed something to Winona where she
> would be a Senate page to a Senator Heather Some-
> thing played by Meryl Streep. Intrigue ensues . . .
> Don't remember much else, except that Christian re-
> turns in Obi Wan Kenobi ghost capacity and Winona
> ends up having to save then assassinate the President,
> which is a good thing. It was all very cwazy [sic],
> but the punchline is that I ran into Winona a couple
> months later and she said, "I talked to Meryl at a
> party . . . and she's totally in!"

A Stop at the Snappy Snack Shack

Amy Poehler on *Heathers'* Influence

Amy Poehler co-founded the Upright Citizens Brigade, spent seven years on Saturday Night Live *(for which she was twice nominated for an Emmy), and has starred in several feature films, including Mark Waters's* Mean Girls. *The mother of two young boys, she also recently re-launched the web series and social networking site* Smart Girls at the Party *(smartgirlsattheparty.com).*

On Mean Girls *and* Heathers*:*

Mean Girls was so funny because the script was so great. And it was filled with great jokes. It hit on the universal message of "what group do I belong to?"

The face-to-face bullying shown in movies like *Heathers* and *Mean Girls* almost seems old-fashioned these days. With all the cyber shit, saying mean things to a person's face is almost charming. The way people can anonymously hurt someone, or systematically spread rumors about someone, is out of control. I would have never imagined that the same girl who tortured you at your locker in school could be the same girl who tortured you in cyberspace. Only she'll go by the name orangeslice27.

On being a parent in this world:

Every girl has a moment in school where everyone hates her.

It's bizarre. It's like a wandering virus that hits every girl between fourth and fifth grade. Trying to figure out why it's your turn is useless. The best thing you can do is keep your head down and be yourself.

That's why I started Smart Girls at the Party. I wanted to create a website that celebrated regular girls who change the world by being themselves—in all honesty, the only artillery that works. We need to encourage girls that whatever they like is cool, whatever they are good at is what they should keep doing, whoever they can be themselves around are the friends they should keep.

The Extreme Always Seems to Make an Impression

The Performances in *Heathers*

As directors go, Michael Lehmann is very hands-off. He is very careful in the casting process, so when the cameras roll, he can stand back and let the actors bring themselves into the part. Patrick Labyorteaux, the actor who plays Ram, speaks fondly of Lehmann's approach: "He would set a shot and then he would read the paper."

The blood, sweat, and tears in the casting process were shed mostly by the actors. Ryder lobbied hard for her role. She insisted she had a personal connection to the script: A girl at her Petaluma, California high school had gained instant, stunning popularity after killing herself, much the way Heather Chandler does in the film. Winona's (soon to be ex-) agent dropped to her knees, begging her not to do the film, but once *Family Ties*'s Justine Bateman and *Labyrinth*'s Jennifer Connelly passed, the role was Ryder's.

Casting J.D. obviously took time. They needed a likable, charming, but believably psychopathic teenager. Two of the sides (script excerpts used for auditions) were from the scene in which J.D. walks in on what he thinks is Veronica's hanging corpse, and the other was the scene in which J.D. and Big Bud greet each other by calling each other their own name. The reasons for picking these scenes are pretty clear: If an actor can handle the mouthful of words in J.D.'s big monologues ("When our school explodes tomorrow, it's going to be the kind of thing that infects a generation. A Woodstock for the '80s!") and dance along to the irony of a boy addressing his father as "tiger," clearly he's worth considering for the part. Slater relishes the dialogue, bringing his now-trademark, then-wait-what-is-this-kid-doing Jack Nicholson delivery to J.D.'s increasingly sinister talk. Lehman recalls being a little more hands-on with Slater initially, questioning the good sense of what sounded just like a *Five Easy Pieces*-era Jack impression. Slater pointed out, "That's how I talk." And history has proven him right. That said, according to a 2008 interview, he did model some aspects of his performance on Nicholson's satanic turn in *The Witches of Eastwick*, a favorite film of Slater's. *Eastwick* had just come out two years before and it ties in nicely with Waters's initial screenplay idea—a high school girl falling in love with the Antichrist. Lehmann nods to this quietly when J.D. introduces the "petition." And his face is framed by the flames of a burning photograph.

The film took the quirky girl from a couple decent movies, found her inner Natalie Wood, and sent Winona Ryder on a course that has included working with some of the great American directors and garnering an Oscar nomination. Her performance in *Heathers* is so informed by her wardrobe (the bruised palette discussed earlier) that she barely has to speak. But speak she does. She has dense chunks of dialogue, all of it overwritten, yet all of it sounding like it just popped into her head. Waters is right to talk about her "wobbly" characteristic. Beautiful though she may be, there's always been an uncertainty about her—and that, coupled with her real-life penchant for dating guys in pretty good bands, has made her geek-bait for the entirety of her career. For a while in the 1990s, it seemed like every third band had a song about her.

Slater and Ryder staged a fake romance while publicizing the film—they even claimed to have been married in Vegas. Their plan was to go further and stage huge public rows, basically tweak the whole gossip machine. Then Ryder became engaged to Johnny Depp, and that era of mischief ended.

Heathers is, in my opinion, unique among '80s comedies in that there really are no weak links in the cast. There are really no small roles in the film, and everyone gets a moment to shine and endow his or her scene with a tiny bit of personality and idiosyncrasy. Lisanne Falk (Heather McNamara) was a teen supermodel with a couple of tiny acting credits to her name, and her performance is wonderfully vulnerable and wounded. She looks like she's barely holding it together in most scenes, and she makes you laugh while breaking your heart in the scene where she calls into a radio advice show (*Hot Probs*). Her attempted suicide, a scene later, and her recovery at the hands of Veronica, gives the film a sincere, irony-free, warm moment.

Kim Walker is positively serpentine in the role of Heather Chandler, and when she spits out, "Fuck me gently with a chainsaw," one has the distinct fear that she could handle it. She's not all sadomasochistic strength, however. After she's been sort of consensually violated by a Remington college boy and she's trying to wash her mouth out, she gives a shattered look into the mirror and spits mouthwash at her reflection. It's a pretty raw and honest moment in an otherwise glib film. It works all the more because Walker had an amazingly aloof look to her, so much so that she played another iconic teenager: On the shortlived TV series based on S.E. Hinton's *The Outsiders*, she portrayed head "soc" Sherri Valance.

Anyone familiar with *Heathers'* DVD supplements knows that Walker—the actress who utters the line, "Did you have a brain tumor for breakfast?"—died of a brain tumor in 2001.

Penelope Milford had earned an Oscar nomination for her role in another film rich with commentary, Hal Ashby's 1979 *Coming Home*, a no-holds-barred indictment of the Vietnam War in particular and macho histrionics in general. It's a fine, nuanced, and nomination-worthy performance, but it gives little indication that she can be funny. And from the moment her Pauline Fleming saunters into frame, glasses on a string, caftan akimbo, she has us laughing at her personal hell that is actually *made* of good intentions. What starts as a sensible attempt to get the teachers to acknowledge the tragedy of suicide turns into a disgusting, self-serving attempt to honor self-destruction. To—as Waters says—"put it on the menu." And the only thing funnier than Milford is the just-wants-to-watch-football principal, with his caustic dismissal, "Thank you Ms. Fleming, you call me when the shuttle lands." The principal is played by John Ingle, who knew a thing or two about being in a faculty meeting—he taught drama at Beverly Hills and Hollywood high schools for twenty-plus years. He retired in 1984 and *then* launched

an acting career. His credits include hundreds of hours of soap operas and a lot of very convincing work in stern teacher roles.

Patrick Labyorteaux (Ram) has one of my favorite takes of the movie. Maybe of all movies. It's a perfectly silent moment during the scene in which he and Kurt confront J.D. in the cafeteria. Kurt asks his friend, "Doesn't this cafeteria have a no fags policy?" Ram stares off into the middle distance, unable to discern rhetoric or irony or really anything that's not right in front of him, his quizzical eyes seemingly asking, "*Does* the cafeteria have a no fags policy?"[19] Labyorteaux was

---

[19] One more thing about this scene: It appears in the excellent 1995 documentary *The Celluloid Closet*, a moving exploration of gay portrayals in cinema, during a montage of film characters using the word "faggot." While I agree that any word can be overused, it should be pointed out that the word is used in this context by two very unlikable characters, who are pretty swiftly punished for their bigotry.

a child star who attended the Valley Professional School, an institution for child performers, both actors and figure skaters (a typical class would star Labyorteaux, Janet Jackson, Corey Feldman, and Brian Boitano). A school filled with drama kids and ice skaters has very few bullies per se, but he still remembers how "Jason Bateman got thrown in the trashcan a lot."

Mark Carlton has exactly one scene as Kurt's dad, but if you're gonna have just one scene, make it the one where you utter a line loved by many: "I love my dead gay son!" The scene works because he's not playing it for laughs: The character's intolerance is on display, and Lehmann wisely undercuts the joke by casting a glance at Kurt's little sister, crying in her pew. The family is broken, but maybe they've grown more sensitive in the process. And Veronica gets to see the real cost of "scaring people into not being assholes," as J.D. puts it.

Another great performance moment comes at film's end, as Veronica begins to put together J.D.'s plan. She stops Rodney (Jon Matthews), one of the geeks, to ask where everyone is going. He tells her the student body is heading to the pep assembly in the gym. *Click.* Her detective hat goes on and she asks, "What's beneath the gym?" Rodney goes through a very quick and mistaken epiphany: If she's asking me about the basement, she must want to fool around down there! With a voice full of hope and as much flirtation as he can muster, he murmurs, "The boiler room . . . ?" Which is just what she fears. And she leaves him standing there in the hallway. I remember passing notes back and forth with girls and wildly misinterpreting them, too (my hand to God, that hot Asian girl in social studies was flirting with me, but it turns out she was really, *really* not). The vain hope in Rodney's voice is so true and pure I practically have to watch the scene through my fingers.

A Stop at the Snappy Snack Shack

The Quotable Daniel Waters

Daniel Waters is an enjoyable interview, and a fun eccentric. He's never learned how to drive, and he lives in a city where that's practically a misdemeanor. And he doesn't live just anywhere in Los Angeles, he lives in the Hollywood Hills house where Orson Welles spent his last years and, in fact, died in 1985. Among the many great quotes the man can offer, here's one he gave to the Los Angeles Times *regarding living in Welles's house:*

"*I wanted to get that* Citizen Kane *mojo. Instead, I'm getting . . . the hanging out with Henry Jaglom, doing wine commercials and magic tricks part of his life. I mean, I enjoy my life, but come on—where's my* Touch of Evil?" *Here's Daniel Waters on . . .*

. . . life after high school:

It is amazing: Obviously there were cliques, and obviously there were people who were made fun of but now, you look at Facebook, and the people who stayed in Indiana, they're all friends, they all know each other. They send each other Starbucks [gift certificates], and it's like, "Wait a minute . . . you can't send . . . He's a *nerd!*"

. . . the public's initial reactions to the film:

People in their twenties and their early thirties, they respond to the movie right away. Teenagers, you know, it was

50/50. A lot of them worshipped it . . . it's the only movie I know that people really like, [but] the first time they saw it, they hated it . . . I don't hear that about any other movie. I've gotten to talk to some of these people, and it's kind of like when you film a child crying and then show the child crying the film—they're not going to be amused by that.

In high school, I was all perspective. I was almost like an avatar in my own high school [*laughs*] but a lot of people didn't respond to it. They thought, "I can't deal with this right now, I can't deal with this right now," and then later on, they came back to it. It's funny, I'm having great romantic success with women who were teenagers when *Heathers* came out. A new skill set!

. . . Heathers' *box office:*

We did amazing in New York. We did amazing in two real theaters in LA. But New World felt that—and New World was really financially strapped—so they released in, like, fifty theaters in LA, which was a mistake. In Rancho Cucamonga, no one's gonna see the movie. If they would have just kept it platform release[20] [*he trails off a little, ruefully*]. And then they couldn't afford advertising. *Heathers* is really funny, because . . . it played in more separate theaters than any movie I can remember. It just never quite left LA. The

---

[20] A platform release is when a studio opens a film in just a few theaters in a couple of major cities to build buzz, and *then* rolls it out countrywide. Recent examples include *Brokeback Mountain*, *Frost/Nixon*, anything that Lars von Trier inflicts on the public.

battle was lost before the army took the field, as far as New World being out of business. They released one other movie called *Under the Boardwalk*, and that was it. That was the ballgame.[21]

If you talked to me ten years after *Heathers*, I was much more bitter—"It shoulda been a hit!" Now (fans will say), "Hey, my God, aren't you lucky that you got to make *Heathers*?" I feel kinda the same way, I'm just happy to get out of Saigon. The fact that we got released is insane, amazing. If this movie was made today, a) it probably wouldn't be made today and b) you know, who knows what would happen to it? There's no New World anymore. [*switches to sage film executive voice*] Independent film is neither independent nor film.

---

[21] In fact, New World made one more film but went under before its release, and sold it off to Triton Picture for distribution. *Meet the Applegates*, directed by Michael Lehmann, was rushed into production before the script was ready, and all parties paid dearly for it. Lehmann has called the experience "humiliating."

Ouch . . . the Lunchtime Poll

The Reaction to *Heathers*

Heathers received pretty mixed reviews upon its initial release. There were the typical outcries, accusations of irresponsibility from squares who were never going to get it in the first place; but even some viewers who should have enjoyed the film, who should have realized it was talking right to them, turned on it. Roger Ebert gave it a lukewarm two and a half stars, asking, "Is this a black comedy about murder or just a cynical morality play?" Now, I like Ebert. A lot. But he's the rare critic for whom you can follow the standard retort, "Well, let's see you write a movie," with, "Oh *shit*, you did"—*Beyond the Valley of the Dolls*—"and it's one of the most

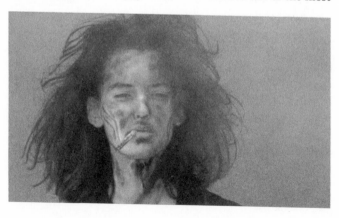

creepily misogynistic films I've ever seen. And I'm including *all other Russ Meyer films.*" Ebert's uncharacteristic cluelessness about *Heathers*—it *can* be both a morality play and a black comedy; most good satires are both—recalls the shrugging reviews given to *Bonnie and Clyde* upon its release[22]. That is, given to that film by most critics, with the notable exception of Pauline Kael. Kael made her mark as a film critic by being one of the few writers who got what the seminal film was trying to do: fuck with our expectations and twist archetypes so far as to make them unrecognizable. Of *Bonnie and Clyde*, she said the film "keeps the audience in a state of eager, nervous imbalance." Waters is thrilled that Kael reviewed his film even though she didn't really like it ("The young, inexperienced director, Michael Lehmann, doesn't find the right mood for the gags," she wrote). That's how much of an unrepentant film geek Waters is; there's a certain tragic "yeah she hit me, but that means she cares" quality about the way he speaks of her review. He also fondly quotes an obscure review from a long dead magazine called *Model*, which read, "Waters is chilling in what he assumes is common ground." What does that say about Waters? (For that matter, what does that say about me? Here I am, trying desperately to convince you of the universality of getting mugged in Ed Koch's New York, and then trying to tie it into a twenty-year-old cult

---

[22] Easy there, movie cop, no one is comparing *Bonnie and Clyde* to *Heathers*. I am, however, comparing their initial critical reactions. Now go back to your dog-eared copy of *Easy Riders, Raging Bulls* and stop glaring at me.

movie that finally made its money back, oh . . . a couple weeks ago? Maybe *there's something chilling about* what I assume is common ground . . .)

Speaking of New York—in its paper of record, Janet Maslin complained about *Heathers*, claiming that the film shifts after the deaths of Kurt and Ram: "It is at about this point that the gorgeous, petulant Veronica begins to wonder just what is going on. And it's at about this point that the film loses its nerve, demanding that Veronica wake up to the awfulness of what J.D. has done." But why *not* now, Janet? Three murders seems like a good time to realize that things have gotten out of hand, and three is a magic number in comedy. Which is to say, with two instances of anything, you establish a pattern (Veronica's unwitting complicity in the murder of Chandler and Ram) and then you break the pattern for shock value, for comic effect: Veronica shoots Kurt dead. It's her point of no return; it makes us gasp. Waters bristles when people accuse his film of copping out at the end, since, he points out, "98 percent of teen movies are a copout from beginning to end."

But if anything, reading the negative reviews has actually strengthened my resolve. Fun-eating *Chicago Reader* film critic Jonathan Rosenbaum is so joylessly dismissive of *Heathers*, you don't know whether to buy him a drink or take him into the woods behind the school and shoot him. Rosenbaum writes, "The real narrative force behind this movie is nihilist camp, as in Roger Corman's 1966 *The Wild Angels* but without the same degree of filmmaking skill." Hang on, Jonathan. Let's not type anything rash. Kick the gun over to me.

Now, I like Roger Corman. A lot. But have you seen *Wild*

Angels recently? I have, and I teetered uncomfortably between ennui and mortification throughout the viewing. It's best not to compare a movie of *Heathers*' craft and deliberate technique to a genuine exploitation film—and I'm using the word as pejoratively as a fan of the genre can—that has not aged as well as you think it has. Somehow a film that contains a scene as offensive as Diane Ladd's rape on a church altar takes *forever* to get there, padding its first two acts with faux badassery and actually making you wish that the tasteless degradation of Laura Dern's mom happened *sooner*. And furthermore, remember the way your parents sounded when they talked about *Wild Angels*? How they thought it was trash and a sign of declining mores? Get their voices in your head . . . and then re-read your review of *Heathers*.

My *Heathers* poster—Veronica and J.D. canoodling over my head as I went to sleep every night of freshman year—had pull quotes from sources as diverse as *Daily Variety* ("The film's sword has many edges, all of them razor sharp") and *Cosmopolitan* ("What will take you by surprise is the remarkably high level of intelligence, humor, and outrage"). People got it, or at least got what it was trying to do, and gave it a lot of points for even attempting it in the era of George Bush the First.

Anything worth writing about is usually decried in its time, and history has been kind to *Heathers*. Just a quick glance at the DVD cover will remind you that *Entertainment Weekly* called it the "best high school black comedy ever made." Which, I guess, ranks it above *Election* and . . . I dunno . . . its pretty lame rip-off, *Jawbreaker*? Sixties cult oddity *Lord Love a Duck?* Hard to say, but *Heathers* is viciously quotable, and it just keeps coming up among people my age. When I casually referred to Sarah Palin as a "mean girl" on Twitter, a friend pointed out how lucky that made us. After all, he said, if she got her shit together, Sarah Palin could be a Heather. Which is a good point about *Mean Girls*. Lehmann was offered the script and wisely passed, knowing that even if he nailed it, it would just look like a retread of his first feature. The film was directed by Daniel Waters's younger brother Mark, whose tuition at the American Film Institute had been paid for by Daniel. It's a solid teen comedy, with some well-observed characters, but with its pedigree and its trio of vicious pretty girls it begs comparison to *Heathers*. And it doesn't quite have the edge. Nor can it afford to: It takes place very much in our world, and if somebody pulled a gun in the movie (or said "fuck me gently with a chainsaw," for that matter), it would feel abrupt and terrible, not broad and satirical. The dialogue is funny, but not terribly stylized, and it isn't trying to be a huge satire of society at large. Grounded though it may be, it's asking the same question: "Why are young women so mean to each other?" Tina Fey points out to a girls' PE class in a preachy but well-intentioned moment, "You all have got to stop calling each other sluts and whores. It just makes it okay for guys to call you sluts and whores."

When discussing his movies, Waters often comes back to the metaphor of the Island of Misfit Toys, a location from the 1964 animated special *Rudolph the Red-Nosed Reindeer*. The misfit toys are just that: trucks with square wheels, a cowboy who rides an ostrich, and their appeal is that they are original, completely their own thing. *Sex and Death 101* is the gun that squirts grape jelly: You don't necessarily need it, but it's pretty cool. "When it comes to cinema," he elaborates, "I feel we live in a world where originality is only appreciated when it's an originality that is completely familiar and comfortable."

Mean Girls. *Juno*. *Gossip Girl*. The *Scream* movies. *Glee* (one of Waters's favorite TV shows). Pretty much anytime teenagers don't sound like teenagers but are still compelling and funny, they ought to send a check to Waters. He cheekily acknowledges that his film is so influential he wishes people "would watch some other movies." There's a terrific rumor he's heard that an Emmy-winning writer once spent a year in therapy lamenting the fact that he'd never write anything as good as *Heathers*. It crawls under people's skin and, in my case, has stayed there for twenty-plus years.

I reached Heather #2 via Facebook. She's moved out of New York, has a good-looking husband and three kids, and initially didn't want to be interviewed. She claimed that she didn't really like the film the one time she saw it (I don't remember why, which shows how much real attention I was paying to the situation). I remember being very nervous, very insecure around her. She did nothing to perpetuate this, but I would clam up around her friends (especially her invariably tall, well-dressed male friends). We bonded initially over movies, and I specifically remember one exchange after we had both seen James L. Brooks's *Broadcast News* over the weekend. We both enjoyed it, and she could not understand how Holly Hunter would be interested in William Hurt when

Albert Brooks was so clearly into her. If I were the sort of person who says, "Wow, I am *in there*," that would have been a great moment for it.

We would go see a lot of movies (*Working Girl*, *Dangerous Liaisons*, *Say Anything* . . . a pretty entertaining year for movies now that I think of it), and, frankly, have a lot of sex (which she always called "making love," a phrase that's just mind-blowing when you're seventeen), but we never really got to know each other. We were from different sides of the tracks: I lived in a teensy apartment in Hell's Kitchen; she lived in a monster brownstone in the East Village. She was planning on going to Europe that summer and wanted to be "free." We looked wildly different: She was beautiful and always well put-together; I was cute at best and seemed to go out of my way to dress terribly. We were heckled on the street once by a young man who asked, a little too loudly, "What are you doing with *him*?" There were, oddly enough, shades of Diane and Lloyd from *Say Anything* in the relationship, only her parents were not stealing from old people and I was not invited to Europe. So, yeah. There was a five month sell-by date stamped on the relationship—and I'm not knocking the experience, it certainly beat seeing *Say Anything* alone, or with any of my long-haired, let's-set-off-firecrackers-in-the-schoolyard friends. But there was also a part of me that, subconsciously or otherwise, didn't see the point in really getting to know this person, this beautiful cipher.

I liked her parents. She had a pool table (she would trounce me every game, and I found it erotic). She introduced me to Cat Stevens, Otis Redding, and Ella Fitzgerald, and I made her a ton of mix tapes and brought her cheap flowers—carnations, as I recall—but I spent most of our torrid senior year protecting myself. And when Josh told Gillian and Gillian told everyone that we were dating, Heather #2 became, to my mind, disproportionately upset. She liked her privacy, and I mine, sure, but I figured, worst-case scenario, a few people who usually ignored me would discover I was *making love* with the hottest girl in the twelfth grade, who was also a member of the National Honors Society and had graduated early due to her excellent grades. Oh, and the entire bottom floor of her brownstone was hers, and as such she was a seventeen-year-old who basically had her own apartment. So suck it, world.

On the other hand, now everyone also knew that Heather #2 was dating that funny guy who used to wear two unmatching shoes ("Nobody else does it!") and wore a red, green, and yellow dread bag over his long, uncombed (but not dreadlocked) hair and had terrible posture and often acted like he was smarter than everyone else, even though he was conspicuously *not* in the National Honors Society. So maybe she had her reasons for being discreet.

Most of the booster ads in the back of our school yearbook were a half-page written by parents ("Mordechai, we're so proud of you." "Congratulations, Yesenia." That sort of thing). Then there were the cheaply constructed pre-Adobe ads from local businesses. Pretty standard yearbook stuff. Heather and her friends (all of whom I knew casually, none of whom I'd ever, say, visited at home) took out a full-page ad, a collection of glamour shots of the school's better looking students just . . . posing in Central Park, framed by trees. In the middle of the page, a group shot and the insipid lyrics of the Terry Jacks hit "Seasons in the Sun" ("Goodbye to you, my trusted friends," etc.). My senior quote, for the sake of comparison, came from the Dead Milkmen: "This world is full of people who think a lot about bowling balls." Neither one is particularly insightful, but there's a lot of real estate between the two sensibilities. On the side of Heather's friends' full-page ad they placed a short legend: "What are we playing? Thumper! Why are we playing? To get *?(!@ up!" Thumper is a drinking game wherein everyone has their own hand signal, and people pass the turn around the table by using someone else's signal. If you miss your signal, you drink. I hated Thumper with an irrational, white-hot passion. When I was straightedge, I thought it was retarded, but even now that I drink—often and with occasional abandon—I just don't get drinking games. Why play around? Why not just drink? I remember writing a short story about a group of teens who get caught playing the game and are taken off to a re-education camp[23]. The Thumper people would often look right past me, as if I weren't there, and stride down the hallways, perfectly coiffed and always wearing their jeans tucked into their socks. And here was my quasi-girlfriend—gone to Europe by the time the yearbook came out—on a page with the Thumper people. Now here's what's weird: I never saw her play Thumper. Maybe she hated it, too? Maybe she wasn't any more "of" that group than I was. Maybe that's why we dated in the first place.

So why didn't she like the film? For a while, I could only

---

[23] Can't find the story. Hopefully, I had the good sense to throw it out.

guess. Heather wore a black scrunchie (*oooh*, what does *that* mean?) and became very self-conscious about it as we left the theater that night in March of 1989. Somebody in the row ahead of us pointed out her hair accessory and she laughed softly, saying, "Yes, I'm a Heather." And the guy turned his finger into a gun and "shot" her. Kinda flirtatiously, if you ask me. So *that* had to be uncomfortable. And as she had just recently ended a relationship with a guy who played football, she was probably not thrilled to see the football players demonized as licentious thugs. But we never really talked about the film, maybe because it was just too weird and close to the bone for her?

I figured all hope was lost. She would not talk to me again, and now I had a sad ending to this book (the Heathers and the nerds can never really be friends, and I am a nerd forever). When I told my wife that I was giving up, she said, "Try her again. Just send her some questions." And when your wife suggests you really, really try to get back in touch with an ex-girlfriend, it behooves you to do so.

I sent Heather one last Hail Mary pass of an email, a couple days passed, and then suddenly she wrote back, with extensive "notes on high school." In a thrilling entry into the "careful what you wish for" file, she also scanned several love letters I'd written to her and sent them to me.

Seems that aside from my anger issues, I was a pretty romantic guy, pretty ambitious, fond of misspelling SAT words (my mom apparently barged in on us at an "inopurtune" moment), and pretty nuts about her in my distant and detached way. A sample quote: "At any rate, have a neat time in Connecticut. I'll probably give you a ring on Friday, that being our anniversary and all." This sentence was followed by eight one-eyed happy faces. That's me in a horrible, horrible nutshell. First off, John, you're *definitely* going to call her, and look at how cool we're trying to sound: "give you a ring." Yeah, John, why don't you drop her a line, toss her a jingle, why don't you guard your feelings in archaic slang? You're crazy about this girl. How crazy? You're commemorating an eight-week anniversary. And then you undercut that with your one-eyed happy faces, your ridiculous "have an unusual day" iconography. Reading these letters is like smelling your own farts times infinity.

Heather and I had had classes together on and off all during high school, but I guess we really started talking in a volleyball PE elective my senior year. As I said to her in a recent email, "I will die wondering how I managed to woo you in a physical education class—especially one where I had to wear plastic goggles over my glasses because I kept taking volleyballs in the face. SEXY." Asked her out and we went to see *The Naked Gun* (funny, sure, but go ahead, find a less sultry date movie), and then went back to her house and watched something else, I want to say *Harold and Maude* (cue the Cat Stevens mix tape she made for me). So she was beautiful *and* she loved the holy writ of quirky teenager movies. She remembers feeling very "romantic and engaged" during our time together. I remember it that way, too, and I specifically recall a long walk near Tavern on the Green in Central Park, after a fresh snowfall, where the ground crunched under our feet and the city kept its voice down for half an hour. She also stuck around when I was incapacitated for a week after having my wisdom teeth out—even invited me over when I had been unable to brush my teeth for a week! Basically our relationship is more proof that J.D.'s thesis—different social groups can only get along in heaven—is simply wrong. Or, at least, simplistic.

A Stop at the Snappy Snack Shack

An Email Interview with Heather #2

Heather #2 lives in the Mid-Atlantic States (since I have to use her real first name, I'm trying to keep this as anonymous as possible) where she raises three really beautiful kids with her husband, a doctor. She taught special education in the local public school district before resigning to spend more time with her children. Among the many revelations she shared in our recent correspondence was the sad news that our high school was closing. After a test-cheating scandal, declining test scores (despite all that cheating, the scores still went down—oy), and a dip in student interest in attending the school, the Department of Education will close the High School for the Humanities in June of 2012.

On public school in general:

My initial response to folks who ask me about high school is that I learned then the immense value of going to school with people who were very different from myself. I had a health class one semester and there was an ongoing exchange of ideas on parenting and culture. I met kids from all over the place and it was fascinating. I didn't love the early dismissals because of gang activities and it was unfortunate that I once had my report card burned out with a cigarette by a loser acquaintance who took issue with my high grades, but it was still an intriguing place. I never got contraband using stolen credit cards, but I was sometimes excited by the low level criminality of a bunch of guys in my homeroom. I had a handful of exceptional teachers who made me excited about learning, and that's a good thing. To this day, I'm committed to public school education for my kids. I know it won't necessarily be the best education out there, but I've realized education takes many forms (e.g. recently when driving by a Red Lobster my seven-year-old exclaimed, "Red Lobster! That's where Jasmine [a classmate] is going when her dad gets out of jail!" There was no judgment, he was just stating a fact.)

On our high school in particular:

High school was hard for me to navigate. I had a good deal of acquaintances, but not many close friends. My sense is that people often assumed I was a conformist at Humanities, but I definitely was not. I did not really fit in anywhere. (I'd be curious to know your recollections of me.) Looking back, it seems strange that I was so out of place. I'm still close friends with Theresa[24] who was my best friend at Humanities. She's really the only person, other than you, who I'm still in touch with. She refuses to touch Facebook—and I understand her distaste. It's fun and entertaining, but also grossly voyeuristic and often vapid. Anyway, Theresa always tried to reassure me that my lack of friends and my inability to relate to many of my peers was because I was an "old soul." I basically skipped a lot of the silliness of adolescence.

---

[24] Name changed.

Maybe that's why I liked and still like silly people like you (by silly I mean people who are easy to laugh and make light of life). My other thoughts on why I had a hard time fitting in are that I can be very shy and self-conscious. College was not much better than high school. At [her Northeastern liberal arts college], I was the nerd at a party school of drunkards. I had a few good friends, and a long-term boyfriend for most of the time, but the social side of college was mostly a drag. In the end I graduated Phi Beta Kappa and President's Fellow—top senior in my major (psychology).

On her recollection of Heathers*:*

Until you reminded me, I had no recollection that you and I had seen it together. I do remember that I never really liked the movie. For obvious reasons, I didn't like that the name Heather was getting such a bad rap.[25] I've always loved my name because it's part of my Scottish heritage and the Scots are proud! My mom picked the name because she said it could never sound harsh even in anger and she had a beautiful image of rolling hills of purple heather. Is it any wonder I love Jane Austen? The other reason I didn't like the film (and this is digging back into my very poor memory) is that it was mean-spirited. I just don't care for mean-spirited stories. I guess we all have our revenge fantasies and they're healthy in their way, but I never got a kick out of that movie.

---

[25] At the time, I remember her saying the film was misnamed: She always seemed to have a problem with girls named Kim.

So there you have it. She wasn't really that close with the group in the full-page yearbook ad. Heather, beautiful, smart, well liked, was shy and self-conscious. She felt, like absolutely everybody, left out in high school. Daniel Waters is quick to point out that when people talk about the movie, they almost always claim to be Veronica. Is it because everyone flatters themselves? Or is it just because we're all a little out of sorts, a little above and a little below the strata we find ourselves near? Do the Heathers all feel like they're Veronicas? Or are we all Veronicas because we simply cannot deal with the fact that we're Martha Dumptrucks?

What a Waste, Oh the Humanity

Aftermath

The Edgar Awards are given by the Mystery Writers of America to works that excel within the crime genre. The term "mystery" is applied loosely: Anything concerning crime and its practitioners is eligible. In 1990 Daniel Waters won the Edgar award for Best Screenplay. *Heathers* is in this pantheon alongside other winners like *In the Heat of the Night*, *Pulp Fiction*, *Silence of the Lambs*, and *Chinatown*. The films just mentioned also won or were nominated for the Best Picture Oscar in their respective years.

The then-very-young Independent Spirit Awards honored Michael Lehmann and Denise DiNovi for Best First Feature. Britain's fun film magazine *Empire* has since put *Heathers* at #412 in its list of the 500 Greatest Movies of all time—nestled between *Spiderman 2* and *Finding Nemo*. And most importantly, people's eyes lit up when they heard I was working on this book. No one has said anything to the effect of, "Huh. Why *that* movie?"

I can't mention an ex-girlfriend without talking about the movies we saw together. Patricia and I saw *Sid & Nancy* on two separate dates. Heather #1: a double feature of *Diva* and *Last Tango in Paris* at a revival house. Annie, the girlfriend after Heather #2 . . . well, Jesus, we saw a million films, we were together nine years before she realized that she . . . well, we saw Rose Troche's *Go Fish* and Sally Potter's *Orlando* together, so that should make it pretty clear what she realized.

But honest to God, I think *Heathers* was the first film that I viewed as a text. That's saying something. I saw *Seven Samurai*, *Citizen Kane*, *Annie Hall*, and *The Bicycle Thief* before I saw *Heathers*, and I guess I viewed them all as . . . entertainment? Even *The Bicycle Thief*. *Heathers* was the first film that said to me: "Wait. This is to be read, chewed, digested, dissected. This is not a passive craft. You have responsibilities that go beyond eating popcorn and cleaning up after yourself. You have weight to pull here, and you can start by figuring out what these colors mean." So, sure it's not the only movie I could write a book about, but it's the first. But still . . . why *Heathers*?

After I graduated from college, I moved back in with my mom in the little Hell's Kitchen apartment, applied for a job at my old high school, got it, and went to work that fall as a teacher. My degree was in English, but English teachers kind of grow on trees, so I taught three sections of English as a Second Language and two sections of Special Education Language Arts. Most of my old teachers were still there, with the notable exception of Mr. Pedroni, whose molestation charges were pending; he'd been put on "administrative leave" at the Board of Ed in Brooklyn. But my art teacher, my old bio teacher, a bunch of the English faculty, all of them were still at Humanities and all of them were incredibly welcoming to a former student who was now a colleague. I got drunk for the first time ever after a grueling, depressing evening of parent-teacher conferences. Where five parents showed up, representing five of my eighty-five students. A bunch of us—my old art teacher, my old science teacher, two of my old English teachers, and me—went down to Jekyll & Hyde, an incredibly cheesy Victorian horror theme-bar in the West Village. It's probably the least gay West Village bar because it's so goddamn tacky. The drinks started pouring (and I had participated in the school's blood drive that day, so I got extra drunk extra fast). Soon enough, the shit-talking started, with the teachers talking smack about hacks who "didn't teach," clicking their tongues at losers who were only still working because they had tenure and bitching about the department heads they called "stupidvisors." It continued at a faculty meeting, where this group (myself included) staked out a place at the back of the library, snickering during the principal's longwinded speeches and rolling our eyes at the teacher with the then-unheard-of habit of carrying a mobile telephone on his belt. (He used it to call the parents of unruly students. In 1993.) There were very clearly cool teachers and not-cool teachers—and the makings of cool were the same at this level. Chalk on your butt? Not cool. Went scuba diving on spring break? Cool. Out drinking on a school night? Cool. Staying in to grade papers? *Nerd*.

Late in the school year, I was told that budget cuts made it impossible for the school to retain me. Just before this news came down, a second-year senior took a swing at me for touching his backpack. If he'd connected, I doubt I'd be able to write anything. So I left the school without argument, de-clined another teaching job in the Bronx, and started a vague, twenty-something life of temping across the city, in horrible, tight-assed offices. I honestly think I temped in every industry the city has to offer: fashion, accounting, pharmaceuticals . . . you name it. I put on a ghastly khaki-and-tie combination and gave them a time sheet. And everywhere it was the same: There were the "cool" partners, the all-too-eager associates, the trod-upon administrative assistants. All of them treated like children by their peers. Which is to say, treated like adults.

I am no closer to finding answers to my questions: Who am I in this film? Why does it speak to me? I met a few football players at camp, but I only had to put up with them for a month. The pretty girls were aloof, but never really mean—not to my face, anyway. New York is its own little world, with unique rules that don't apply elsewhere in the country. Again, I took a date to the opera. And that was . . . sort of . . . cool?

The film is a satire, and the characters are broad and silly. Most cult movies deal with broader archetypes; any stern, highbrow essay on *The Rocky Horror Picture Show* will illuminate this idea better than I ever could. We're not supposed to see ourselves directly in *Heathers*, just see heightened versions of our tendencies. We're all Peter Dawsons and Heathers and J.D.s and Braces. And it doesn't matter. I have been asking the wrong question.

It's less "who was I?" than "who will my daughter be?" She's almost four. We're raising her in Los Angeles. My wife and I have to be here for work, since our skill set (acting) is less useful in, say, Detroit or Memphis. It's a status-conscious city,

Los Angeles, and I worry that my daughter will fall under the Yellow Box shoes of her peers. Or whatever the fashionable shoe will be when she starts high school in 2021. Will she be a Betty Finn, caught up in her studies, loveless? A Martha Dumptruck, so hapless that she botches a suicide attempt? Or worse, will she be part of the problem? Will she be wearing the future hot shoe, pressing it into the scalp of those beneath her? Right now, she's sweet, incredibly articulate, and very gentle. But she's also a manipulator: She'll call through the baby monitor, "Mommy, I want to sit on the couch." When that doesn't work, she tries a different tack: "Mommy! I want a kiss!" Does this foreshadow future devious behavior? Getting people to forge notes for her? Ruling the school with an iron fist closed over French tip nails?

And my son, younger by two years, is a brute. A smiling, funny brute, already more mobile than my daughter was at this age. The way he beats at my wife while she's breast-feeding makes it look as if her chest owed him money. Chess and checkers. It's never an issue of what world they are going to inherit; it's what world are they going to create. I don't really want her to be an actor. I don't really want him to be a writer. But I want them to be happy and fulfilled and excited to get out of bed most mornings. I want what every parent wants: for my children to have better, more stable, less terrifying lives than I did. I want my daughter to have friends that she can trust, to date guys or girls who loan her good books, and I want her to get drunk exactly once in the eighth grade, pay for it with a devastating hangover, and then never touch the stuff again until she's in her twenties. I don't want her to kill or be killed, but she should absolutely, 100 percent kill if the choice is binary, and I don't want her to fall for "bad boys," perceived or otherwise. I want him to be picked early for teams, and to stand up straight, and to never, ever raise his hand in anger against a woman, and to tear up at the end of *Cinema Paradiso*. And I want them to know that I will absolutely love them no matter what, even if they violate every edict I've just laid down. For a while there, when my daughter went to bed, I would do something that my wife made me stop doing: I would whisper, "I approve of you," so that she'd never make any decision based on the feeling that she didn't have her father's approval. My wife found this creepy.

And will I be able to show them *Heathers*? To prove that their anger is normal, but that its end result—the revenge fantasies that they naturally harbor—are counterproductive, absurd, and ultimately laughable? Or will there be other ways of showing them? The hopes of a *Heathers* sequel are squashed ("fed liquid drainer," according to a *Movieline* headline from 2009), but plans for a musical based on the film continue apace. Songs have been written, readings have been staged. It's freely adapted from the film, but not so free that you won't recognize it. Act Two has a rousing gospel number called "My Dead Gay Son."

I'll Repeat Myself

Seth Walsh, a thirteen-year-old in the small town of Tehachapi, California, just south of the slightly larger town of Bakersfield, had been pulled out of his junior high in order to be home-schooled. The harassment and bullying that he faced by being an out-of-the-closet teen had grown to be too much. But leaving school apparently didn't help. You probably know the end of this story by now: Seth went home after one too many days of being insulted on the playground, hung himself, and died nine days later. The news, of course, got worse. In this age of the twenty-four-hour news cycle, suicide proved nationally contagious, and within the next month, four more gay teens had killed themselves.

As of this writing, bullying of all sorts is being seriously addressed in high school campuses across the country, in what seems like an unprecedented . . . what? Rise in concern? Outpouring of empathy? Bullying is a vaguely defined term, and is not illegal, just a cruel part of social Darwinism that can run rampant when unchecked. The kids who hassled Seth Walsh, the kids who badgered Asher Brown until he shot himself in the head in Texas—not criminals, any of them, just misguided pricks with absentee parents. There is no legal recourse, but I'm comforted by the preventive quality of the "It Gets Better" videos. When celebrities from Ellen DeGeneres to the sitting president of the United States get on TV to tell harassed kids, from the other side, that this bullying is temporary, that it is born of the inadequacies of the bullies, it might carry more weight than any sort of judicial deterrent. As the ending of *Heathers* hopefully, if satirically, extinguishes the flame of high school class war, just maybe these videos and testimonials will bring the perspective that is so needed when it seems as if the world and all of its inhabitants are closing in on our heads.

That said, there is an apparent need for such solace to be accompanied by a really mediocre pop song. The "It Gets Better" tune that closes George Takei's consoling, foul mouthed PSA is the sort of mundane folk pop that proves what we all fear: Life might not always be high school, but the world will always speak to high school students the same way.

Bibliographic Information
and Acknowledgments

First and foremost, my gratitude goes to the good folks who consented to be interviewed for this book: Michael Lehmann, Daniel Waters, Patrick Labyorteaux, Amy Poehler, and the two Heathers.

Other quotes come from the two documentaries on the *Heathers* DVD, "Swatch Dogs and Diet Coke Heads" and "Return to Westerburg High." Also helpful was the *Creative Screenwriting* podcast interview with Daniel Waters, conducted when he was promoting *Sex & Death 101*. Around the same time (2008), the *Los Angeles Times* published "How Very," an interview with Waters. Thanks also to the women of the horror site pretty-scary.net. I also cited "A Woman Friendly Guy," an interview with Lehmann during the promotion of *Because I Said So*, and other Lehmann interviews that appeared in *V Magazine* and *Movieline*. The smart website enjoy-your-style.com has a well-observed article on the "fashions" of *Heathers*.

The Criterion Collection edition of Douglas Sirk's *All That Heaven Allows* brought a great deal of insight to the table, particularly that great quote about art and trash. I'd read Steven Levitt and Stephen J. Dubner's *Freakonomics* years ago and happened to remember the section on girls' names. It holds up nicely. The BFI series on films, the 33⅓ series on beloved records, and a great book called *Unruly Pleasures: The*

Cult Film and Its Critics (Fab Press, 2000) provided phenomenal inspiration. There's a whole chapter in there devoted to a heated, unironic, and unapologetic defense of *Showgirls*. It's utter horseshit, but a great read. My love of film aesthetics and analysis comes from the class of that name that I took with Professor Frank J. Tomasulo. The good doctor runs the film nut site mubi.com, where you can discuss and even watch rare films, and which I really cannot recommend enough.

The less fun acknowledgements: Dave Cullen's book *Columbine* and some of his attendant interviews. I also cite *The Surgeon General's Call to Action to Prevent Suicide* from 1999, and a CDC paper, *Epidemiologic Notes and Reports Cluster of Suicides and Suicide Attempts*, which offered great insight into the Bergenfield County suicide pact mentioned herein. Two books, *Suicide and Homicide Among Adolescents* by Paul C. Holinger and *Adolescents' Health: A Developmental Perspective* by Inge Seiffge-Krenke, offered valuable psychological information and telling statistics.

Thanks must go to Sean Howe for thinking of me for the Deep Focus Series, and for his tireless editing and his patient assistance with my apostrophes. Ditto the editorial staff at Counterpoint. Eternal thanks to Jamie for her encouragement, love, notes, and, as ever, for noticing things I don't.

For Nola and for Walter: If you are happy every day of your life, you won't be human. You'll be a game show host.